Early

Canadian Pottery

Donald Webster

McClelland and Stewart Limited *Toronto / Montreal*

0-7710-8930-9

The Canadian Publishers
McClelland and Stewart Limited
25 Hollinger Road, Toronto 374

Printed and Bound in Hong Kong

Contents

Foreword

One only has to compare the extensive bibliography on English ceramic history with the sparse list of publications on Canadian and American ceramics to realize the value of a new book on early Canadian pottery. Donald Webster has brought to this project a rare combination of professional skills. As Curator of the Canadiana Department of the Royal Ontario Museum, Mr. Webster, on a day to day basis, is involved with a wide variety of objects related to Canadian material culture. This strong background in Canadian antiquities is combined with his special interest in historical archaeology; he has excavated a number of Canadian pottery sites and has published scholarly reports on his investigations. Thus, two related disciplines have been brought together to produce this much needed volume.

Two aspects of Mr. Webster's book merit special comment. First, the object itself always holds centre stage. Many ceramic historians, especially those of the old school, concentrate heavily on documentary source materials. Such scholarship, of course, often provides much valuable information – but sometimes the ceramics themselves are neglected. In this book the ceramics *are* the basic source materials. The result is a clear-headed objective approach that seems especially useful in penetrating the hazy, romantic, legend-filled atmosphere surrounding so many collectors and dealers. At times the truth hurts, and there are some painful truths in this book.

The second aspect of Mr. Webster's work that should be mentioned is the use of archaeology as a research tool. Potters were often secretive people, protecting their recipes and techniques by keeping most working data in their heads. Further, many of the early potters probably verged on illiteracy, and record keeping was sketchy at the best. Thus, as this generation of ceramic historians is discovering, properly conducted archaeological investigations in many cases provide the very best insights into the history of long-dead potteries. Usually the waster piles yield reliable indicators of a pottery's output. Mr. Webster's archaeological evidence is, in many cases, new and important.

Early Canadian Pottery is needed, a welcome addition to the half filled shelf of books on North American ceramics. This volume is for serious students of Canadian social history and material culture. It also is for ceramic historians. And, equally important, it is for the many collectors and dealers who, in their particular ways, do so much to help in preserving objects from Canada's past.

J. Jefferson Miller II
Curator of Ceramics History
National Museum of History
and Technology
Smithsonian Institution

Colour Plates

page 9

French terrines vert, green-glazed bowls of buff earthenware, roughly turned without finish smoothing. Only the interiors and rims are glazed. A stack of seven of these bowls was excavated beside the foundations of a late 17th century house on Ile d'Orleans, Quebec, where they had probably been intentionally buried. Diameters, Left 12⅞", Right 12⅝".

Three Quebecois utility bowls, the smaller two with pouring spouts, and all transparent lead glazed only on the interiors. The lower right piece is the earliest, c. 1770-1800; the other two date c. 1800-30. Diameters, Left to Right 10¼", 15", 9".

page 10

Bowls and serving baking dishes, all red earthenware from the Dion Pottery, Ancienne Lorette, Quebec, c. 1870-1900. All are brown spattered and transparent overglazed, some with a tinge of copper-green. Diameters/Lengths, Left to Right, Rear 14⅜", 9⅛", 11⅞; Front 8¾", 8¼", 10¾".

Four Ontario earthenware pitchers, the centre two finished in a typical Germanic manner (one stamped P. BAILEY), both c. 1860-80. The outer pieces, Rockingham glazed with brown slip spattering, are somewhat later, c. 1875-1900. Heights, Left to Right 7¾", 8⅝", 6", 6¾".

Three milk-skimming bowls from the Maritimes, all of dense red earthenware, and finished and glazed only on the interiors. The rear bowl, lined in white slip and overglazed, is a common form made at several potteries, this one from Nova Scotia, c. 1870. The left black-lined bowl is a rare type, also from Nova Scotia, c. 1870. The right-hand piece, with dripped white slip decoration, is from the Prince Edward Island Pottery, Charlottetown, c. 1880-90. Diameters, Left to Right 15½", 14⅝", 12½".

page 11

Tall earthenware jar, with a strong Ontario-German influence, olive-green glazed, and mottled orange by flecks of iron oxide sprinkled on the still-wet glaze. From an unknown Waterloo County, Ontario, pottery, c. 1850-75. Height 18¼".

page 12

Ontario-German earthenware miniatures, with a Brantford salt-glazed salesman's sample, c. 1875-80, at lower left. The miniatures, all small replicas of larger forms, are from various potteries of southwestern Ontario, c. 1865-90. Heights 2" to 4".

Moulded earthenware King Charles Spaniel, coated with white slip, spattered with brown, and with a collar and leash painted in cobalt blue, all underglaze. Made at the Samuel Burns Pottery, 1871-84, Markham, Ontario. The finished dog is flanked by two identical biscuit-fired and unfinished pieces excavated at the Burns Pottery in 1968. Heights 8¾".

Ontario-German special exercises, at left a toy rocking chair made of rolled and cut slabs of clay cemented with slip, c. 1860-80. The chair is coated with yellow and red-brown scroddled-slip, underglaze, a rare finish on Ontario pottery, and perhaps an attempt to simulate English agate-ware. The covered sugar bowl is decorated with yellowish-white slip bands and spots, the spots then covered with mocha-like diffusions of brown slip, and transparent overglazed. Southwestern Ontario, c. 1880; very similar sherds were excavated at the William Eby Pottery, Conestogo, in 1968. Heights, Left 6½", Right 5" (incl. lid).

page 13

Seven-gallon salt-glazed stoneware crock, with an incised decoration of two birds and a coggled band, filled with blue glaze. The crock is stamped F. P. GOOLD & CO./BRANTFORD, C.W. Incised decorating is usually associated with American stoneware of the 1810-40 period, but was done on a few known Brantford Pottery pieces during Goold's ownership, 1859-67. Height 14½".

page 14

Brantford Pottery stoneware picture frames, cast or pressed in a single mould, and made c. 1862-63. The left-hand brown slip coated piece is unmarked. The right frame, with an excellent Rockingham glaze, is marked on the back in incised script, "G. BEECH/MAKER/BRANTFORD/1863". Heights, Left 12", Right 12¼".

Slip-cast Rockingham-glazed teapots from the Brantford Pottery, both c. 1880-83. The left piece, with a "Rebecca at the Well" relief pattern, is equipped with an excavated lid. The right-hand piece is the beaver and maple leaf pattern. Neither piece is marked. Heights, Left 5", Right 6".

page 15

Baking dishes from the Charles Pearson Pottery, Iberville, Quebec, c. 1880. The dishes are identical, and marked C E P on the bases; though one is Rockingham and the other yellow-glazed. Lengths 11⅜".

Yellow-ware bowls of the 1870-80 period, banded with white and brown slip, with two pieces also decorated with mocha-diffusions. The large left bowl and the small foreground reconstructions are from the Brantford Pottery; the centre and right-hand pieces are from the Cap Rouge Pottery. Diameters, Left to Right 11⅝", 6½", 8¼", 5", 9½".

page 16

Late 19th century pitcher and washbowl set, with a green Rockingham glaze over stoneware, and marked BRANTFORD/ CANADA on the bases. Brantford Pottery, c. 1894-1906. Diameter, Left 13½"; Height, Right 11½".

Ironstone china, all from the St. Johns Stone Chinaware Co., St. Johns, Quebec, 1873-93. This company was the only 19th century producer of ironstone, and all pieces are marked on the bases. The white-wares are the most commonly found type; the blue ironstone is quite rare. Heights, Left to Right, 3½", 6", 7", 3", 7½".

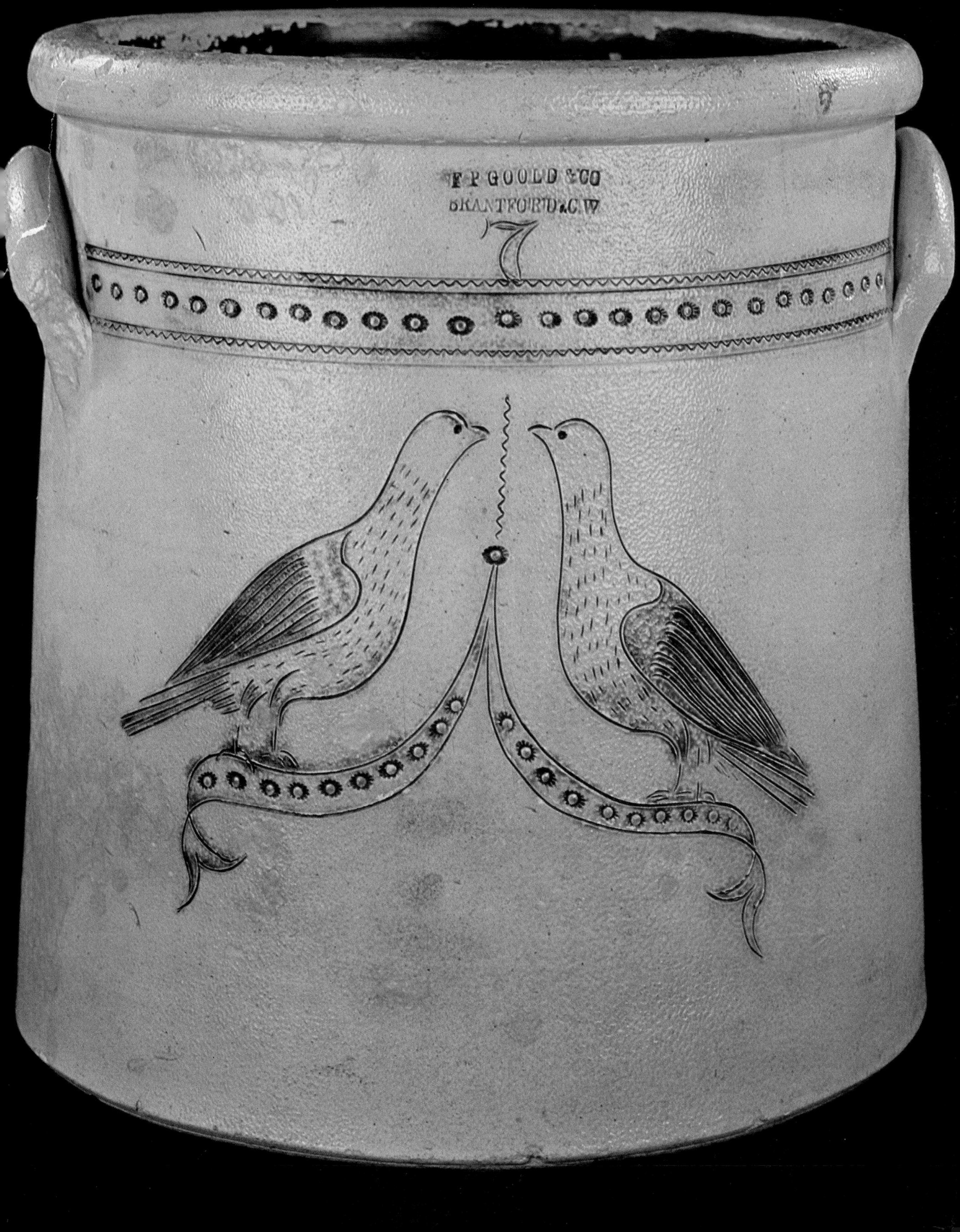
F P GOOLD &CO
BRANTFORD.C.W
7

Introduction

Ceramics, as vessels of fired clay, have for thousands of years perhaps been closer to the domestic existence of people of all civilizations than objects of any other man-formed material. Utility pottery – containers and utensils – were so ubiquitous a part of the daily stream of life in Europe and North America before 1900, and still are in some areas of Europe and most of the rest of the world, that their production and presence were very much taken for granted. The finer and more artistic wares alone, the products of the master ceramicists, were noticed in their own time. Only through hindsight does the real role and necessity of utility pottery – essential, if not to human survival, at least to all facets of human convenience – become evident.

Over the last half century in much of the Western world, newer materials, notably mass-produced glass and plastics, have filled many of the functions which ceramics earlier served. The rougher and more basic types of pottery, the earthenwares and stonewares, thus replaced, have largely disappeared. Unfortunately, particularly in North America, the ethnic and regional decorative arts which embellished much of this pottery have likewise vanished.

Canadian pottery is a relatively recent focus for the attention of collectors, and only very recently has it received any real attention. Part of the reason for this may be that ceramics collectors, until lately, were largely oriented solely toward object aesthetics, with little appreciation of the historical, technological, or cultural manifestations of their subject.

No early studies exist on Canadian ceramics, and this lack of previous specialized work and publication makes some core problems blatantly apparent. Above all, how do we determine just what pottery is Canadian in origin and what is not? And then, once we know or at least suspect that a piece is in fact Canadian, the question rises of making attributions to a specific area or a specific pottery or factory.

Anyone collecting Canadian ceramics is faced with the fact that until quite recently Canada was a colonial environment with a colonial economy; and perhaps it is not yet fully past this phase. As a distinct cultural entity, the country was growing and developing by the 19th century, but at that time it had neither the capital, in the sense of money, skills, and equipment, to create a modern industrial establishment, nor the population and the internal market to support one. This meant that, at least until well into the 20th century, a very high proportion of the physical objects necessary in any society had to be imported. Ceramics were no exception.

There is little doubt that before 1900 the great balance of pottery and other ceramics used in Canada was brought in from Great Britain. This importation included virtually all of the finer ceramics—tablewares of ironstone or porcelain whose manufacture required a sophisticated industrial base—with the only Canadian-made exception being the ironstone of the St. Johns Stone Chinaware Company, whose production was miniscule when viewed against the total stream. Native or indigenous pottery production, then, was restricted by the economic facts of life to earthenwares, made from naturally occurring clays and in scattered small establishments, most of them individually or family owned.

Early Canadian pottery can be roughly divided into two main groups. First, both chronologically and in numbers of makers, are the coarse earthenwares. These were most typically containers or heavy table utensils, formed of local red or buff-firing clays, and made by hand in small commercial craft potteries with few if any mechanical aids. The second and later group comprised the mechanically-formed or industrial pottery, slip-cast or press-moulded household pieces and tablewares. In this group are the factory produced Rockingham-glazed and relief-patterned pitchers, teapots, and other hollow-wares, and the yellow-glazed and banded bowls, all of the later 19th century.

The few existing early pottery factories operated simultaneously with the earthenware craft potteries until the early 1900's, and in a few cases as late as the 1920's, but were making substantially different types of wares. Their days, however, all were numbered, first by a changing domestic environment and market that provided less and less demand for pottery containers, long the mainstay of the industry. Finally, these potteries and factories were ultimately doomed by the obsolescence of their materials — red earthenware and natural stoneware. Neither was

as suitable for making finer wares, nor as adaptable to industrial mass-production techniques, as the processed and artificial whiteware clays already long in use in English and American factories.

To collectors the period from 1850 on is usually the most interesting. Prior to the mid-19th century very few potteries in fact existed in Canada, and all of these were small operations with a very limited production of a few simple utilitarian forms. In the decades after 1850 came a spurt of growth in the industry—both an increase in the number of craft potteries, and the beginnings of the industrial or factory period. It was during this era that the greatest variety and quantity of pottery was produced in Canada.

As the craft potters in the later 19th century tried to expand their commerce beyond the limits of container-ware production, myriad forms of earthenware appeared. The industrial potteries at the same time marketed an increasing range of moulded wares, based generally on forms, fashions, and finishes which were then popular in the United States, but also sometimes copied from English imports.

The great majority of this pottery is completely unmarked, thus raising the problems of identification of just what is or is not Canadian, to say nothing of attribution. The collector of Canadian ceramics, then, has no choice but to concentrate on developing his eye toward overall perception and recognition—an instinct of experience—rather than depending on markings. Positive attribution of unmarked pieces to specific potteries is difficult (and as of now often just not possible), particularly when considering simple containers and utility vessels.

It is not my purpose in this book to offer a precis on every pottery in operation before 1900, or capsule histories of all potters. That has already been done, and excellently, in Elizabeth Collard's *Nineteenth-Century Pottery and Porcelain in Canada*. This book, rather, is intended to outline and illustrate for collectors the range and variety of the early Canadian pottery itself—as collectable antiquities. It will thus suffice to mention the major or better known producers in conjunction with examples of their surviving products.

Some appreciation of the potting process, and of materials and methods, is essential to developing the instinctive eye. I have therefore included a section on the technology, both crude and otherwise, that produced the pottery of the 19th century, so that the collector may better understand the objects with which he is dealing. The book is also written using basic ceramic terminology, which is specific and not particularly complex, and a glossary of terms and definitions is added at the end of the book.

Surveying an area such as Canadian pottery, unexplored till very recently and not yet really fully sorted out, is spadework in more ways than one – what we might call first generation research. The methods involved, both for documentary identification and tracing of potters and particularly for connecting the pottery itself to the potteries, are both varied and fascinating. In the hope that some ceramic historians and collectors find the chase as exhilarating as the catch, I have included a final chapter on the means employed in gathering information (and some experiences) both on the potters and their enterprises, and on the pottery itself.

1 The Production of Earthenware

Pottery basically is nothing more than clay formed into some specific shape, allowed to air-dry, and then fired or baked to a permanent hardness. Clays of different types, and from diverse localities, usually have different components in varying proportions. Clays thus will fire to a multiplicity of colours or states of fusion and hardness, but clay in one form or another occurs naturally everywhere on earth. When formed into vessels and fired to a proper temperature, it forms a completely permanent body which is not subject to corrosion, decay, or dissolution. The universal occurrence of clays, and the basic simplicity of making from them useful objects of a permanent material, is perhaps sufficient reason for pottery always having been man's basic utilitarian container in all human cultures and over some thousands of years.

Pottery container wares, completely aside from imported English table china, were extremely important throughout early Canada, largely for producing, conserving, or storing food. During the 18th and most of the 19th century the food preservation methods we now take for granted did not exist; vacuum canning was not in widespread use before the 1860's, nor refrigeration, with ice, before the 1870's. Most modern food processing, packaging, shipping, and distribution systems were also unheard of before the 20th century. Before this each family unit, whether growing or raising its own food, or buying it in urban markets, had much more individual responsibility for processing, preservation, and storage than would typically be the case today.

Because of the primitive state of processing and marketing, and of the limitation of preservation techniques (particularly before the advent of home canning) to drying, pickling, and salting, the basic household required a wide range and quite some number of heavy containers. Ideally these had to be rugged, and particularly they had to be inexpensive. There were, of course, wooden barrels and tubs for liquid or dry storage, hand-made by coopers, relatively costly, and limited in possible shapes and sizes. Barrels soured, leaked, got sprung, rotted, and though fine for bulk transport were hardly suitable for universal household use. Metal cannisters were also available, made of sheet iron, crudely tinned, hand soldered, likewise expensive, and subject to leaks, punctures, and rust. Glass was difficult to make, for larger than bottle-sized vessels were typically hand-blown; in shipment and in use glass was subject to a high degree of breakage, and it was also expensive.

Without an industrial establishment capable of massive and relatively automated production, the day of the truly disposable (i.e., far less expensive than its contents) glass, metal, or ceramic container was a long way in the future. What the ordinary household needed was flexible or general-use containers, readily available in various shapes and for different purposes, heavy enough for hard usage, yet cheap enough to be acquired in some numbers and for breakage to be no great domestic disaster.

As it always had been, earthenware was the obvious answer – locally fabricated of a raw material which cost nothing. Pottery, as simple containers, was remarkably easy to produce. A small pottery-making establishment required little if any cash investment, for the physical plant and the productive raw materials were largely a matter only of labour. Clay was free for the mining, though it invariably required cleaning before use. The pottery vessels could be turned out in quantity; a skilled potter could form a simple piece to completion in less than a minute. Glazing was then simply a matter of dipping an air-dried or once-fired pot quickly into a liquid glaze mixture.

The pottery was finally baked or fired in brick domed kilns, usually large enough to hold a week's or a month's production of a potter. Firing called for two to four days of constantly tending wood fires, twenty-four hours a day, first slowly increasing, then maintaining, and finally slowly decreasing the temperature within the kiln.

Finally the kiln was unloaded and the finished pottery, if all stages of the operation had gone well, was ready for distribution. The pots were often sold directly from the pottery, and also by the wagon load to small general stores or crockery shops. The country potter was perhaps more directly concerned with marketing as well

Essentially a large vertical mixer, the typical earthenware pottery pug-mill was used for breaking up lumps of clay and mixing with water. After mixing, the refined and fluid clay was removed, screened to remove stones and lumps, re-dried, and stored for use.

Handling several hundred pounds of clay at a time, the pug-mill was typically horse-powered, with the horse pulling a horizontal beam attached to a vertical shaft, the latter arranged with horizontal blades or paddles to pulverize and mix the clay as the centre shaft rotated.

Earthenware container pottery was wheel-turned, and each piece shaped by hand. The only aids were ribs and scrapers for forming curves and rims, and height and width gauges for uniformity.

as production than was the urban producer, who sold most of his wares to wholesalers or other distributors. The marketing area of the rural earthenware potter was usually quite small, rarely extending more than twenty or twenty-five miles from the pottery. Prices varied, according to the size and complexity of wares, but even large crocks seem to have sold for less than a dollar a dozen, and smaller containers went for as little as three cents each.

No potter, whether he ran a one man shop or owned a small factory, ever became wealthy. The industry was competitive, for though any given potter might have a relative monopoly in his own area, he could hardly charge more for pottery than a producer in a neighbouring area, lest his customers go elsewhere. The technological crudities of most early potteries also assured that not every pot that successfully left the potter's wheel actually made it to market; the quantity of pottery lost during production was often rather high.

Earthenware pottery began its life as raw alluvial clay, usually a grey or blue-grey in colour as it is found naturally, and generally filled with dirt, small stones, and other impurities. Once laboriously dug, probably too dry and stiff to work, the clay was mixed with water to the consistency of a very thick cream, another exhausting job. A pug mill in Canadian potteries served as a mixer, consisting of a wooden tub or barrel with a spiked shaft mounted vertically in the centre, the shaft attached to a horizontal overhead beam. A horse harnessed to the horizontal beam simply walked in a circle, slowly rotating the spiked shaft on the same principle as a modern blender. The effect was to break up lumps and mix with water several hundred pounds of clay at a time. Once fairly fluid, the clay was both hand-picked and screened through wire meshes, to eliminate lumps, pebbles, sticks, and whatever else would be a less than beneficial additive to a pot. The clay was then partly re-dried in the open air and stored until use in tubs or crocks.

The whole process of mining and refining clay was back-breaking work, for the clay was extremely heavy and had to be hand dug, transported to the pottery by wagon, and then broken into usable portions and cleaned virtually by hand. The potter worked with lumps of clay,

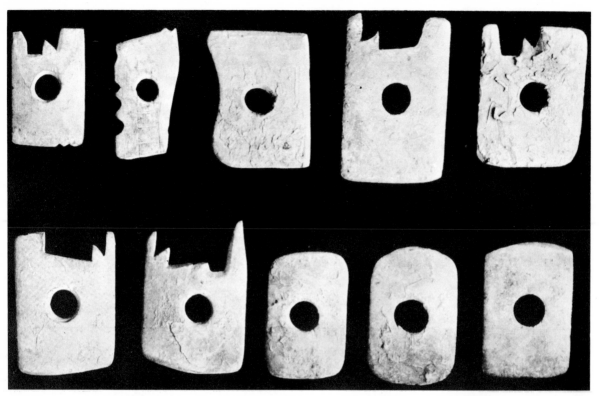

Ribs, small wooden scrapers to shape a particular angle or curve, were a timesaver to the potter and essential to high-volume production. Simply whittled out, ribs could be made in the pottery, and cut to produce virtually any shape.

To achieve uniformity in container pottery, the potter weighed clay for each pot, so that each identical piece produced would ultimately contain the same amount.

stiff and rubbery, both in the preparation stages and in finally forming pots. The demands on wrists, arms, and shoulder muscles were considerable, and for this reason virtually all commercial potters were men, and usually men of considerable physical strength.

The potter who actually formed pottery was known as a thrower, the name originating from his practice of forcefully throwing a lump of clay onto the surface of his potter's wheel to be sure it would stick. The potter's wheel was, and is, simply a round table one to two feet across, mounted on a vertical shaft. The surface was rotated either by kicking a larger lower wheel at the base of the shaft or, more ideally, by an apprentice or a child on the business end of a drive wheel and belt arrangement. Most modern potters prefer electrically rotated wheels, though several types of foot-operated wheels are still very much in use.

The thrower, turning his wheel, would start forming a vessel from a lump of clay, wetted or dried as necessary to the right consistency for working. If, as was likely, he was making a number of identical pieces, for speed he used wooden scrapers known as ribs for forming reasonably identical rims and difficult curves. The batches of clay for forming identical pots were usually weighed in advance, so that for consistency exactly the same amount of clay was used for each piece. To assure identical sizes and capacities, rough wooden gauges determined height and diameter.

From the original lump, the thrower in a minute or so would cut another finished jug or crock from the wheel with a spatula or wire loop, which left characteristic marks on the base. The pot would then be placed on a shelf or a long plank and perhaps marked while it was still wet. In this case the thrower or an assistant, simply using a stamp made from lead printers' type set in a wooden block, would impress the pottery's name and address (or on order perhaps the name and business of a merchant) into the still malleable clay, usually just below the rim. Any stamped or impressed, but not hand-inscribed, decoration would be added at the same time.

Once filled, two people carried the plank and row of new pots out into the sun to dry. An eye was always turned to the sky and wind, for freshly turned pots were still raw clay – rain could turn them back into lumps. Shelves in a warm indoor area were perhaps more desirable. Larger potteries and factories occasionally had indoor low-temperature drying ovens, but these were not typical. After a few days of sunny or at least dry weather, the pots were air-dried, albeit still plain clay, and now called greenware.

At this stage any incised or inscribed decoration or marking that was to be added would be scratched into the dry clay. The usual tool was a small pointed stylus, though a fine-bladed pocket knife would do as well. Incised decoration is quite uncommon on Canadian earthenware, but pieces are occasionally found with markings of the pottery scratched or incised in the base. The pottery was now ready for glazing, if the glaze was to be only a simple surface coating, or for a first or biscuit firing if decorating and glazing were to be more complex.

All earthenware pottery except stoneware is unvitrified. That is, the clay particles are not fused together by silica and the fired pottery is porous to liquids if not glazed. Stoneware or porcelain clay, conversely, has a higher silica content than most eathenwares, is fired at much higher temperatures, and even unglazed stoneware or porcelain is vitrified and non-porous. All of the red-firing earthenwares, however, fired at temperatures of 1300 to 1500 degrees Fahrenheit, require a glaze as a sealer on at least the inner surfaces of vessels.

The glazes used on all early Canadian earthenware were essentially a form of glass, the prime components being silica from ground flint or white sand, lead oxide, a flux such as borax, and gum arabic as a binder, to make the liquid glaze mixture stick to the pottery. The metallic oxide or salt in a glaze determines colour. Lead oxide or red lead alone, and without impurities, will provide a transparent glaze after firing. Copper, depending on the percentage added to the lead, after firing gives anything from a greenish tint to a deep green colour. Iron oxide (powered rust) will give reds, oranges, and yellows. Manganese provides a black, and cobalt oxide, usable only at stoneware firing temperatures, a rich blue.

All of the colouring oxides used by earthenware

Coggle wheels, much like kitchen pie-crimpers, were often used to impress one or more decorative bands as a still-wet pot turned on the potters wheel. Coggling simply required holding the wheel, with a design carved or moulded in, lightly against the revolving pot, with care that the end on the impressed band lined up with the beginning.

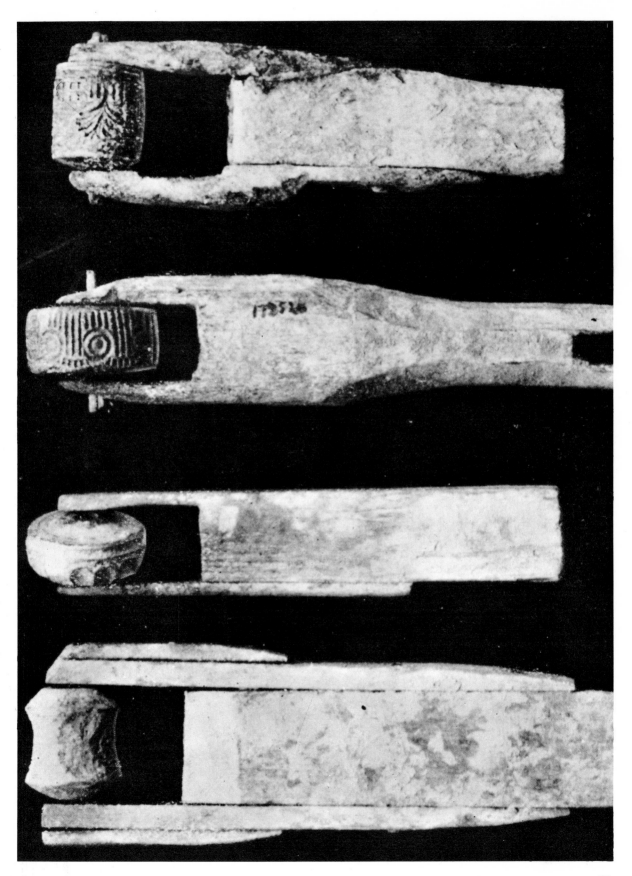

Glazing was accomplished by dipping formed greenware quickly into a liquid glaze mixture. If only the inside of a pot was to be coated, glaze would be poured in, quickly swished around, and poured off. The process had to be accomplished quickly, lest the glaze liquid soften the unfired clay.

Stilts and wedges,—kiln furniture for stacking bowls and plates for firing. On the left are pressed earthenware stilts and hand-formed wedges excavated from the Prince Edward Island Pottery (c. 1880-95); on the right yellow-glazed hard earthenware stilts from the site of the Cap Rouge Pottery (c. 1860-1900), Cap Rouge, Quebec.

potters, added to the always basic lead oxide and other ingredients, still provided a transparent or at best a translucent glaze, through which the colour of the fired clay was still apparent. Only tin oxide makes an opaque glaze, white if used by itself in combination with lead, or softer colours if used in addition to one or more of the other colouring oxides.

Most glazing oxides could be bought in powdered form, but as likely as not commercial supplies were simply not available to the average small craft potter. Not only was his range of colours thus limited, but he had to make his own glazes from materials at hand. The prime component, lead, usually came from the lead-foil lining of tea cases. This was first heated, and then ground to a fine powder. Copper could be obtained from any available scrap, but often was old copper sheeting from roofs or ship or boat bottoms. Copper was treated in the same manner as lead – burned and ground fine. The easiest component to find was iron oxide – any rust scraping or scale would do, and a mortar and pestle was sufficient to render this into a glaze powder. As in many such operations, of course, the heavy work of glaze grinding was often done by children, for child labour was also training in the craft, and the potter's progeny were often involved.

Lead and copper or iron sufficed for most glaze mixtures, for rarely did an earthenware potter attempt to use anything more complex or more sophisticated.

The glaze components were usually mixed in water and the pottery then dipped, or glaze was poured into a pot, swished around to cover all the interior surfaces, and then poured out. Glaze mixtures had to be stirred continually, for none of the components were readily soluble in water and, at best, the glaze mixture was a colloidal suspension.

The glaze was then allowed to air-dry, becoming a fine powder on the surface of the pottery. It was the firing stage that then melted and fused this powder into a glossy and impermeable finish.

If the finish was to be a simple lead glaze, earthenware pottery was often glazed as

greenware, and the clay pots with their glazes given only a single firing. If, however, the glazing was to be more complex, if there was to be slip decorating under a glaze, or if there was any combination of materials in the covering glaze that required firing at a substantially different temperature from the clay of the pottery itself, then the pots were fired a second time for finishing.

Completely unfinished pottery, or pots with slip decorating added over the air-dried clay, were usually biscuit-fired (first but preliminary firing) at maturing temperature, to harden the pottery and slip in the same operation. The glazing was then added and the pots again baked, usually at a somewhat lower temperature, in a second or glost firing. Extremely complex and sophisticated European pottery could on occasion require as many as four or five separate firings, but no early Canadian pottery required firing more than twice.

Slip decorating or slip coating was very common on all Canadian pottery, and consisted of nothing more than a decoration or covering with a liquid clay of contrasting colour to the body of the pottery itself. Slip is essentially a fine clay mixed with water, to the consistency of cream or paint. Since slip is mixed from natural clays, its colours are earth colours, usually white, buff, or brown. Slip clay must also be very fine in texture, thoroughly refined and without granular impurities, as it is both the body and the pigment of a decorating medium. This liquid clay is then applied to freshly formed and dried pottery, either by dipping as with a glaze, by spattering of drops from a brush or stick, or by drawing lines or decorations with a brush or by trailing through a hollow quill or straw.

Slips on pottery should not be confused with glazes, though components of the two were sometimes combined. Slips are clay, and were used largely on eathenware because they could be fired to maturity at the same temperature and in the same firing operation as the pottery itself. Glazes, based on silica and coloured by metallic oxides, form a hard glasslike surface. Slips after firing are still a clay surface, and provide a glossy or non-porous coating only in special instances. Thus slips, where they were used on Canadian earthenware, were generally overglazed whenever they were used as a surface finish.

After a sufficient quantity of formed, glazed, and dried
pottery had been accumulated, it was loaded into the kiln
for firing. Kilns typically were of brick, either cross-draft
rectangular or updraft beehive types, and wood fired.
An earthenware kiln held from 2,000 to 5,000 pots, often
a month's production.

Firing was the most critical operation, and usually the one in which most losses occurred. Most Canadian earthenware potters seem to have used domed or beehive kilns, built roughly of brick, and often earth-covered for additional insulation. These were updraft kilns, with fireplaces at the base, and openings or chimneys at the top of the dome to create a draft and for smoke to escape. Such kilns were fired through two or four wood-fueled fireplaces evenly spaced around the base.

Some potters, particularly in the earlier 19th century, used rectangular cross-draft kilns. These were rectangular structures, with the fireplace or firing opening at one end of the kiln, and the exit or chimney at the other. In such kilns, the flow of heat and of gases was horizontal rather than vertical.

The fireplaces were usually simply openings into the kiln interior, so that direct flame and very often smoke could come into direct contact with the pottery. This led to unpredictable firing, temperature differences and fluctuations within the kiln, and discolouration of clay, which often mandated the discard of at least some of the pottery.

Why kilns of this crudity, without muffling or any structural separation of fireplaces from pottery chambers, were often used we do not really know. Potters were not in the habit of keeping or leaving descriptive records. It appears, however, that many Canadian craft potters, never having worked in areas with an older and more established pottery industry, simply did not know from firsthand experience how to build a proper and efficient kiln. Rather they learned by vague tradition and word-of-mouth, and wound up building what they could simply and cheaply, which was good enough as long as it worked.

Kilns were filled with pottery, stacked up for firing through the fireplace entrances. Stacking had to be most carefully done, the pots separated and the stacks stabilized with small ceramic shims, tiles, and separators called stilts or wedges. It was essential first that pots not touch each other in such a way for glazes to become blemished or fused together. Stacks also had to be stable and arranged so that the pottery would

neither collapse nor the weight of pieces uppermost in the kiln crush the lower pieces. A kiln, of course, was loaded to hold as many pots as possible – one kiln load could represent a month's work of a potter.

The firing process was begun by starting light wood fires in all of the various fireplaces and bringing the interior kiln temperature to about the boiling point of water. This evaporated off whatever atmospheric moisture was left in the air-dried pots. Too rapid a temperature buildup could cause sudden steaming of this moisture, and result, at the very least, in pressure cracks and fractures in the pottery.

By gradually adding dry wood, the fire tender then slowly raised the kiln temperature, as he looked at the pottery occasionally through an opening in the kiln wall. At maximum or maturing temperature, about 1300 to 1500 degrees Fahrenheit for most red earthenwares, the pottery became slightly incandescent and glowed a dull red. If the kiln became overheated, the pottery turned bright red, and beyond that a glowing yellow. At this stage the dried clay became plastic – slightly molten – and the entire kiln-load could sag and collapse into a mass of twisted and distorted pots. This was not an uncommon accident.

Firing temperatures were difficult to judge and more difficult to control, except by eye and experience. There were no thermometers and no measuring instruments. The most ideal conditions were clear and nearly smokeless fires, and a strong draft. Smoke buildup in the kiln was another hazard of firing, from a low draft or damp or resinous wood. This created what is called a reducing atmosphere – reduction of oxygen – as opposed to a more desirable oxydizing atmosphere. Reduction firing caused darkening of the pottery body, often from the desired orange or dark red to grey or nearly black. Glaze colours were also severely distorted either by reduction or by over-firing.

Most firings took two or three days of continual fueling and round-the-clock attention to the kiln, with much of the last day spent in gradually lowering the fires for slow cooling. Finally, the finished pottery could be withdrawn – barring accidents, anything up to two or three thousand pieces.

If the firing had not gone well, the results were shovelled out and simply dumped, most often near the kiln, but perhaps hauled away in wagons. Once fired, pottery fragments, unlike glass, were not reusable. The commercial craft pottery was a messy operation, and the pottery grounds hardly neat.

We cannot really judge the proportion of the total production lost in firing in early potteries, but accidents were most certainly not uncommon. Most pottery dumps or waster heaps reached prodigious size over a period of years – a source of grief to the potters, but certainly a great benefit to present day archaeological investigations and analyses.

The early craft potters, making a scratch living at best, and beset by gradual losses of markets, cultural changes, and technological advances they could never have understood, died off one by one over a generation of time. Their craft and vocation were obsolete, their wares were no longer needed by 20th century society, and thus the sons who tried to follow the fathers typically lasted only a few years.

And so the earthenware potteries closed, most between 1890 and World War I. The pottery itself, or that of it which survived the environ-ment which depended on it, remained, and largely does so today, thanks to collectors. Only a few major producers, however, lasted through even the earlier stages of 20th century technology, and these, notably the Dion and the Farrar potteries in Quebec, lasted only into the 1920's.

They are all gone now, the strong-armed potters, the fire-belching kilns, the fragment-covered grounds, and even the buildings, long since torn down for their materials. The pottery, in some cases, was more durable than the potters, and is fortunately yet with us, though largely without connection to its origins. And thus to the ceramic student and collector, the long ago abandoned pottery establishment again becomes supremely important, though now as an archaeological site.

This story, the process of technical information gathering which has contributed heavily to this present section, must wait until the final chapter.

2 Quebec — The French Period

The earliest Euro-Canadian pottery was the small quantity of utility ware produced in New France, largely to alleviate periods of shortage in the supply stream from France. The pottery produced thus included only a few of the most universally used forms, the types which most often needed replacement. It must be remembered that though New France began its existence as a French-settled colony early in the 17th century, earlier than most Anglo-American occupations, it never achieved the independence of distance of a true colony, in the sense of developing a real internal economy or any significant native manufactures. New France was in no way self-governing.

Although there was a minor internal mercantile establishment, the prime focus was always on the fur trade, managed and mismanaged in an elitist European manner. Virtually all consumer goods and hard necessities came from France, really more in the nature of supplies than of true imports. We must also consider that the total population at the time of the English conquest in 1759-60 was only some 65,000, and the greater part of this consisted of the residents of Quebec and Montreal.

Pottery-making in New France, and even well into the 19th century, was very much a subsidiary occupation which never involved more than a few potters at any given time. The reason for this was perhaps twofold. First, there were never in New France so many European residents as could not reasonably be supplied from France. The early settlers in fact evidently refused, or at least declined, to use Indian pottery, except in situations of desperation. There is no evidence that Indian pottery in any way ever influenced early Quebec pottery, or for that matter any other Canadian pottery.

Second, there was little or no available capital for the setting up of native industry and certainly no official encouragement. There was, in fact, reason to believe that, except for granting permission or license for functions absolutely necessary to any society, both the French government and the governors of New France prohibited establishment of productive industry to keep the population dependent on the home country.

Dinner plate of buff earthenware, lead-glazed on the interior.
Quebec, late 17th or early 18th century. Found in the house of
Jean-Louis Fornel, c. 1723, Quebec, during restoration.
Diameter 8⅝".

Good clay was difficult to find, as potters discovered early, but that was a relatively minor matter. The best clay supplies accessible to the centre of settlement were located along the St. Charles and Lairet Rivers, just north and east of the City of Quebec.

The known existing documentary evidence of early potteries is extremely fragmentary, and no potteries at all appear to have operated in New France before 1690. In 1688 an agreement had been signed, and then quickly terminated, between Gabriel Lemieux and the Governor of New France, but the earliest actual establishment is one assumed to have been started by Lemieux in 1694. Another potter, named Vital Martel, then went into business, again by permission, in 1700.

Virtually all of the earlier potteries were set up along the banks of the St. Charles or the Lairet, in Charlesbourg, now a suburb just east of Quebec. The potters, from mentions in early documents, limited themselves or were limited by the governors to the production of a few simple forms — large utility bowls (terrines), table plates (assiettes), and serving platters (plats). These vessels were made of the relatively fine earthenware of the area, which after firing becomes a light red or a reddish-buff in colour. The pottery was usually lead glazed, generally on the interiors alone, over a wash of brown slip. A few known pieces seem to be glazed over a buff slip, with a lead glaze containing a trace of copper providing a greenish tinge. In the French manner, the exteriors of earlier Quebec wares were usually left unglazed, until in the last quarter of the 18th century a few bowls appear glazed overall.

Pottery-making was a secondary craft even to most of the potters themselves; it was not by itself an occupation at which one could make a reasonable living. The demand and market were far greater for brick and earthen tile, so the potteries apparently concentrated their prime energy and production capacity on construction materials.

The definitive separation of early Quebecois from imported French pottery, during the French period, is still a questionable business, for no one has yet located any pottery site of the pre-1800 period that is presently unoccupied and

Red earthenware utility bowls, with pouring spouts, and lead-glazed only on the interiors. All are mid-18th century pieces excavated from various sites in the Quebec City area.
Diameters 9-10″.

available for archaeological work. Thus we cannot, as an absolute certainty, identify all early Quebec pottery, and we cannot yet begin to identify particular pieces with specific potters, except in rare cases where the context of discovery justifies an attribution.

The existing known pieces of colonial Quebec pottery and the similar imported French types are, as might be expected, virtually identical in form and shape. However, most imported French common utility pottery of the period was densely copper-green glazed over a buff or nearly white earthenware, the latter often coarse in texture. Other common French wares were lead-glazed over the same body, resulting in a medium to dark honey colour.

There is no substantive evidence that any early Quebec-made earthenware was ever green-glazed, or lead-glazed, in this manner. The French wares, well known from numerous archaeological recoveries, in general also have lighter body colours than those the Quebec clays produced. The only pieces, however, that we can presently and reliably presume to be of certain Quebec origin are the cruder brown slip lined, translucent lead-glazed, or somewhat green-tinged bowls, all with definitely reddish or red-brown body colours. All else is still supposition.

In dealing with the pottery of 17th and 18th century Quebec, therefore, there are still a great many unanswered questions involved in what could or might have been. This pottery is quite rare in private or museum collections, and obviously little of it now exists. Documentation is scattered and very sketchy at best, and no early pottery sites have ever been examined.

The early utility bowls, with pronounced rims and rudimentary pouring spouts in the French fashion, seem to be the most common form. The age of these bowls is perhaps best judged by rim configuration. The earliest forms, made presumably during the French period, had heavy overlaid rims, formed by rolling outward the clay rim as a bowl was shaped and smoothing it down to overlap the exterior. Such rims are often deeply undercut, with a readily visible seam. Bowl types of the later 18th century had simplified rounded or everted rims, usually no deeper than their width and without undercutting. In the 19th

Utility bowl of buff earthenware, the interior lead-glazed, found in the Jean-Louis Fornel house, Quebec. This bowl was probably made c. 1755 at the Fornel Pottery, Charlebourg, by Francois Jacquet. Height 3¼".

Utility bowl with pouring spout, the interior lead-glazed over brown slip around the rim. Probably made by Francois Jacquet at the Fornel Pottery on the Riviere St. Charles, Quebec, c. 1752-55. Found during restoration of the Jean-Louis Fornel house in Quebec. Diameter 9".

century, finally, though bowl shapes remained unchanged, the vessel rims became more rudimentary rounded bands. Rims were eliminated altogether on some later bowls, with upper edges of the walls simply rounded off.

These early bowls can still very occasionally, and expensively, be found. All of the known or apparent French colonial versions, however, as well as the very few table or dinner plates known to exist, are archaeological reconstructions, and for the most part are in museum collections. If the early potters of New France, as documents seem to indicate, once made large platters or chargers, of for that matter, mugs or cups, none have yet been found even in archaeological excavations, and most certainly none now survive anywhere intact.

From the beginning of New France until after 1850, a period in excess of two centuries, it appears that a total of not more than a dozen potters operated in New France and Quebec. The Quebec pottery which collectors most readily find today, and in great quantity, although it is made of red earthenware in fact dates from the industrial period — late in the 19th century or even into the 20th.

Utility bowl with pouring spout, buff earthenware lead-glazed on the interior. Quebec, late 17th or early 18th century. Found during restoration of the Jean-Louis Fornel house, Quebec. Height 3½".

Covered jar with integral carrying handle, of red earthenware dark green-glazed both inside and out. Though found in a long-term Quebec context, this piece may be French, c. 1750-60. Height 7⅞".

3 Quebec — The Later 18th and 19th Centuries

Until the beginnings of the industrial period, effectively 1860, pottery-making in Quebec had changed very little from the French period. A handful of potteries provided the same limited and basic earthenware forms as a century and more earlier, but in the 19th century merely supplemented dominant English rather than French imports. The pottery, like most other craft products, was still ethnically quite French, and showed little if any influence either from the growing English population or from imported English ceramics.

By the third quarter of the 19th century, most of the few commercial craft potteries in Quebec had already disappeared — the business had always been tenuous — completely unable to compete with importations or new industrial development. Quebec and Montreal had become primary seaports and population centres. English ceramics, and other goods, landed there were so readily and inexpensively available to the bulk of the population that it was virtually impossible for native craft producers to survive except in remote and sparsely populated areas.

The primary and the most commonly surviving form of the early 19th century was still the standard angle-sided utility bowl, with a pouring spout in the traditional Quebec manner, and brown slip lined or lead-glazed only on the interior. It would, in fact, be difficult to differentiate a Quebec bowl of 1725 from one of 1825 except for its rim for, as previously mentioned, the rims alone became gradually simplified over the years.

There is no doubt that the survival rate of all Quebec earthenware made before 1870 has been extremely low, though certainly more utility pottery was produced than is now apparent. Still, the Quebec population must have depended almost entirely on imported English wares for storage vessels and tablewares, and these are still commonly found. I have yet to see, however, a piece of Quebec-made earthen tableware from any context datable between 1760 and 1860 or so, or for that matter any closed or stoppered container vessel. Such pieces are also rare even as archaeological finds in sites of the pre-industrial English period. English brown stoneware, conversely, is common even today. We can only conclude that, like the Maritimes

Four utility bowls of the late 19th century, without formed rims, but all with the characteristic Quebec pouring spout. The top bowls are lead-glazed overall, from unknown Quebec potteries, c. 1860-75. The lower pieces are green-tinged and speckled with orange, probably from the Dion Pottery, c. 1870-1918. Diameters, Top, Left 8⅛", Right 8¼"; Bottom, Left 9⅛", Right 8¼".

during the colonial period (to 1867), except for an economically insignificant native production, English ceramics totally dominated the Quebec market.

Though documentary searches have confirmed the existence of a number of potteries during the late 18th and first half of the 19th century, all appear to have been craft operations producing a very limited variety and a great sameness of pottery. The range seemed to include only the brown utility and milk skimming bowls, and simple jars and crocks, with few attempts at any sort of innovation or development, and nothing that could be remotely considered as ceramic artistry.

The earlier potteries were concentrated near the sources of clay, the Quebec-St. Roche-Charlebourg area on the St. Charles River, St. Denis on the Richelieu River, and Montreal, with other establishments scattered. One of the longest-lived, perhaps, was the establishment of Antoine Bertrand at Charlebourg, which operated from before 1760 to about 1810. Pierre Vincent, father and son, worked at St. Roche from about 1790 to about 1810. Alexis Cloutier at St. Roche also spanned the turn of the century, operating into the 1830's. At St. Denis, potteries had operated from the 1760's, but Simon Thibodeau, who started his operation in 1776, was probably the most important, with both the largest pottery and the longest span of operation, to after 1825.

As during the French period, however, documentary records are sketchy and incomplete, and some potteries of English colonial Quebec have probably yet to be discovered. Also as in the French period, there is little doubt that virtually all potters were engaged in other more fiscally secure pursuits, most commonly brick and tile-making. Numbers of brickyards, recorded as such in tax and land records, likewise occasionally produced rough pottery as well, and these we may never be able to identify. (The same was also the case later in Upper Canada.)

Even before Confederation and the decline of English mercantile dominance, the industrial period had begun in Quebec, along the St. Lawrence and Richelieu Rivers. The first of the new ceramic factories seems to have been the

Farrar stoneware establishment, started about 1841 at St. Johns, and related in Chapter 7. This was followed shortly by other stoneware factories, and the Cap Rouge Pottery manufacturing Rockingham and yellow-wares after 1860, but none produced red earthenware and none were essentially Quebecois operations.

The last, longest lived, and by far the largest of the earthenware potteries was the Dion factory at Ancienne Lorette. First established by Jean Dion as a small pottery about 1855, the operation grew slowly, and brother Antoine Dion took over the business about 1870. The factory during the next few decades produced a great range of utility wares, ethnically French even at this late date, of local red-firing clay, but also drew on the new technology to produce red-earthenware moulded and slip-cast wares. Though their level of product sophistication was certainly limited by their material, the Dions at one time or another turned out just about everything that could be produced in earthenware, including some superb special and experimental pieces.

Antoine Dion's four sons joined the firm at various times in later years, and managed it and a subsidiary pottery until 1918. The factories were finally closed only when even the rural markets for obsolete earthenware finally disappeared.

Pottery emerged from the Dion factories in vast quantity, and is still commonly found in Quebec antique shops. It is easily recognizable, for both wheel-turned and moulded wares were almost invariably spattered in brown slip over the dark-red-firing clay. The Dion pottery is also glazed on all surfaces, unlike the interior-only glaze of earlier bowls. Often, as well, the Dion glaze contained a bit of copper, resulting in olive-green patches overlying the brown spatter.

Quebecois earthenware pottery, though quite rare before the Dion period, like furniture and architecture retained its essentially French character as long as it was produced, perhaps good evidence of the tenacity of the Quebec culture. It was never made by either the number of producers or in nearly the quantity of Ontario earthenware, but pottery of the earlier periods is still occasionally found, and is perhaps the scarcest single type of Canadian ceramics.

Redware flower pots with integral saucers, the exteriors with brown slip spatter under lead glaze, and the insides unglazed, Dion Pottery, c. 1880-1920. Diameters, Left 7¼", Right 10½".

Washbowl and pitcher, with brown slip spatter under an overall lead-glaze, from the Dion Pottery, c. 1880-1920. Bowl, diameter 12⅜"; Pitcher, height 8¼".

Light redware vessel, probably a kitchen colander with a single line of holes above the base, acquired in central Quebec. The interior is washed with a white slip; the outside is lead-glazed only. The shape is most unusual, though the piece is certainly Canadian, of the late 19th century. Diameter 11⅞".

Baking or serving dishes, spattered with brown slip not well refined or mixed, giving a granular appearance. The spattering covers both exterior and interior surfaces. The body is of an unusual clay which fired to a pinkish color under the lead overglaze. Quebec, late 19th century. Lengths, Left 10⅛", Right 10¾".

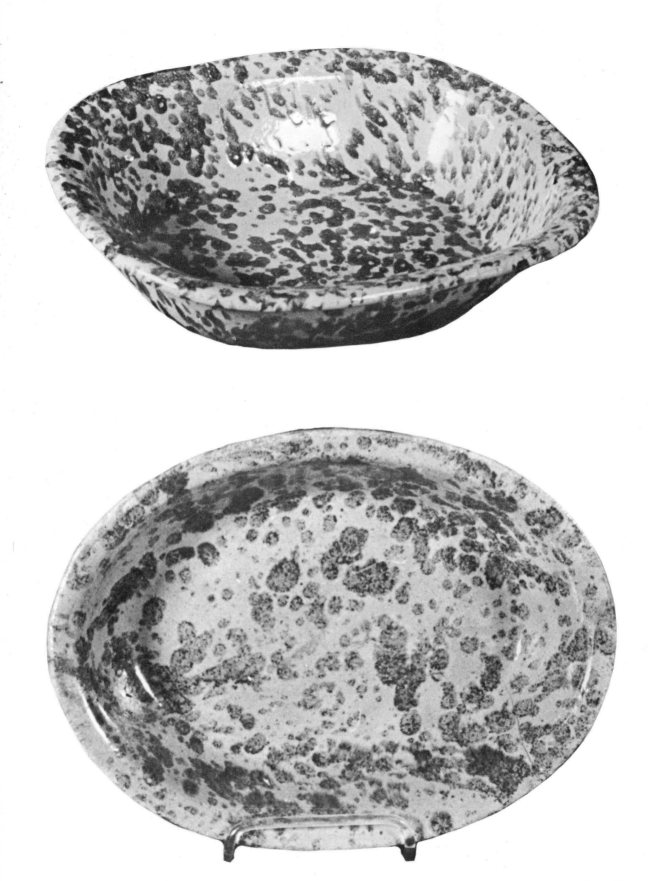

4 Ontario Earthenware

Upper Canada or Ontario, in the mid and later 19th century, had more commercial potteries in operation than the rest of the country combined. Though no potteries are known to have existed in Upper Canada before 1800, and few before 1840, by 1860 there were well over two dozen in operation, and by 1875 nearly sixty. Most of these potteries were individually or family owned craft-based operations, dependent on the manufacture of red-earthenware container and utility vessels, distributing to local markets, and technologically isolated – not really quite in the main stream of the ceramics industry. Yet, in many ways, the Ontario earthenware potteries, by numbers alone, formed a strong cottage industry, and one that prospered until nearly 1900, perhaps largely because of a uniquely favourable marketing situation.

Ontario potters, unlike those in Quebec or the Maritimes, had the good fortune of being geographically separated from direct sea transport, and thus one stage removed from the direct landing of English imports by the rapids of the upper St. Lawrence River. Montreal was a primary summertime port for ocean-going ships, and a terminus for cargoes destined west and coming directly from Europe. Then, however, cargoes for Upper Canada were trans-shipped for a hazardous trip up the St. Lawrence, in earlier years by bateau or Durham boat, and later in the century by small steamers, on to inland and Great Lake ports.

However it was transported, pottery was heavy, bulky, and fragile. Overland freighting on the miserable roads of the period was even more hazardous than boating to fragile merchandise, as well as being of limited capacity and prohibitively expensive for bulk cargoes. Rail shipment from Montreal to Toronto became possible only after 1856. Boat freight, far easier under any circumstances, was by comparison only difficult, but sufficiently so to prevent English imports from dominating the market for at least the cheaper and more basic utility pottery and container wares.

Rural Ontario, the bastion of the craft potters, was yet more difficult to reach with low-priced imported ceramics, for barrels or boxes of boat-shipped pottery landed at a lakeshore town often then had to be reshipped by wagon to

Typical Ontario earthenware types and shapes. Left to right, a York Shilling crock, with green and speckled orange glaze; Covered preserve jar covered with over-glazed brown slip; Cream crock with a dark metallic green-black glaze; Covered jar with mottled light olive-green glaze and iron-red specking and veining; Large jug with orange-brown transparent glaze, and a handled bottle with orange brown transparent glaze over brown specks.

inland villages. There was no effective native competition for English white tablewares, but the Ontario earthenware and stoneware potters found they could reasonably control their own markets for container wares and, until very late in the century, undersell similar imports.

The typical Ontario earthenware pottery concentrated on producing simple and inexpensive products, usually in a limited range of forms, always from locally mined clays, and often without competition, for a geographically local population. As mentioned, these wares were generally sold at the pottery, or in wholesale lots to nearby general stores, but rarely was earthenware shipped any great distance from its pottery of origin. The potter's craft was hardly lucrative, and large agricultural land-holdings suggest that in some and perhaps many cases pottery-making was a part-time occupation, carried on largely in the winter, with farming taking up the warmer months.

The majority of the earthenware potters active in Ontario were of Pennsylvania-German origin, often descended from Mennonite loyalists, or Germans who emigrated from Europe in the 1840's and '50's, with smaller numbers of Anglo-Americans, English, and Scots. Many of these people, and particularly the Pennsylvania-Germans who had been emigrating to Upper Canada since the 1780's, sometimes had generations of the potting craft behind them. Both family and ethnic pottery-making traditions, if not necessarily personal individual training, were very strong.

The earliest Ontario-German potter yet recorded was Jacob Yeigh, of an ex-Pennsylvania loyalist family, who started a small pottery at Burford, Canada West, about 1805. Yeigh served in the War of 1812, and then resumed operations, apparently producing simple container earthenware until the late 1830's. We do not presently know his work, and have not yet located the exact site of his shop.

John Kulp, born in Pennsylvania, immigrated to Ontario and was operating a pottery at Grimsby, in the Niagara Peninsula, by the early 1840's. Kulp's heaviest production was also containers, to suit the widest market, but he is also known to have made a number of toys and miniatures,

An early red earthenware utility bowl, with the interior lead-glazed but no exterior glaze. The bowl is attributed as being one of the earlier products of John Kulp, Grimsby, Ontario, c. 1840. Diameter 7¼".

Earthenware utility bowls of the pre-1850 period. The left rear piece is lined with white slip, and over-glazed, and the foreground piece in brown slip. The exteriors are unglazed. Central Ontario, c. 1830-50. Diameters, 13".

and a handsome redware inscribed jar. Kulp died in 1874; his pottery is not known to have operated after. The Kulp Pottery was excavated in 1965.

Other German and Mennonite names dominate the whole period of commercial earthenware production—Jacob Ahrens, who came from Germany and was making pottery at Paris, Ontario, by 1860; Xavier and Joseph Bochler at New Hamburg in the 1870's; Nicholas Eberhardt at Toronto in the 1860's; William Eby, potting first in Markham, and then at Conestogo by 1857, who operated until 1899 and whose pottery was excavated in 1967 and '68. Daniel Orth, at Campden in the 1850's and '60's; Abraham Roszel, John Kulp's son-in-law; Henry Schuler at Paris and Brantford in the 1870's and '80's; and the Wagner family of Kitchener from the 1850's into the '80's—all made pottery which is known today and can be identified with them, as well as always the high-volume but anonymous and unattributable crocks, jars, and jugs. These people, many of whom potted for long periods, were not by any means the only Germanic potters in Ontario—they were simply representative of the whole cultural and ethnic stream, and are regarded as the most important.

Pennsylvania potters in the 18th century, many of whose progeny later immigrated to Ontario, had produced elaborate slip and scraffito-decorated wares in an old-world Germanic tradition. Increasing travel, migration, and consequent environmental blending of people in the 19th century, however, eroded the earlier ethnic distinctions of the Germanic pottery. Earthenware came generally to be less craft or craftsman oriented, and more a routinely and mass-produced, purely commercial, commodity.

The age of industry and technology advanced in North America very much at the expense of the craft system, for technology demanded the conformity of the product to the means of production—to the manufacturing techniques. Individual potter-craftsmen found themselves caught up, if not directly by the industrial system itself, at least by severe economic competition from the products that emerged from it. Thus primarily artistic and decorative considerations first declined and finally disappeared.

The earliest established dated piece of Ontario pottery, a 2 gallon dark redware jar glazed with the typical Germanic copper-green and iron-red mottling. The jar is incised on the base "JOHN KULP/GRIMSBY/AUGUST 19th/1843." Height 14".

Redware jugs from the Ontario-German area, c. 1850-70. The small piece on the left is glazed with iron-red mottling and veining over a soft apple-green. The larger jug is coated with a dark brown slip. Neither piece is marked, but both are forms and finishes common to many rural potteries of southwestern Ontario. Heights, Left 7", Right 11½".

Tall Ontario-German jars in unusual forms, from southwestern Ontario, c. 1840. Both jars are of red earthenware, the left piece glazed with mottled orange and green, and that on the right covered with chocolate-brown slip. Heights, Left 12¼", Right 8½".

1 gallon earthenware jug, uncommonly decorated with a pattern of sponge-applied brown slip over the clay body. The maker is unknown, but the jug is from one of the earlier Germanic potteries of Western Ontario, c. 1840-50. Height 11".

Both the industrial competition of the factory system, and the household pottery needs of early Ontario, dictated ultimate simplicity, universal forms and shapes, and minimum cost, for the production of earthenware to survive at all. We find, by the later 19th century, that the national and cultural or ethnic traditions of the individual potters were still reflected in some of their products, but now only in minor details and very diluted form. Thus the exotic influences on Ontario pottery became typically quite mixed. Only in some cases was it still possible to sort out the main derivations – the Germanic, the English, and the Anglo-American.

The influence of the English and Anglo-American potters in Ontario generally was more centred in urban rather than rural areas, and these potter-entrepreneurs were also somewhat more industrially oriented than the Germanic earthenware craft potters. The Toronto area, for example, was dominated by English and American potters; the earliest was Thomas Humberstone, who established a small pottery in 1813, making plain earthen container and storage vessels. Though the pottery location changed, the Humberstones, Thomas, Thomas Jr., and Simon, ran the business until about 1915, the longest lived single pottery operation in Canada.

Among several establishments in the later 19th century, the Davis Pottery was important in Toronto in the 1870's and '80's, and continued into the 1920's. John Brown, who started his potting years at Bowmanville, shifted to Toronto and worked during the 1860's and '70's.

The more industrially minded, men such as Justin Morton, F. P. Goold, and William Welding of Brantford, the Harts at Picton, and William and Robert Campbell in Hamilton, are discussed in successive chapters. These were the people who brought the factory system into the Ontario craft-pottery scene, and who both introduced new materials and particularly new production methods.

The manner of glazing pottery can be essentially indicative of its underlying tradition. In Ontario the Germanic potters typically used a basic lead oxide glaze containing other colouring oxides. After firing, this produced translucent glazes which were often mottled combinations

Ontario-German small red earthenware jug and jar, both glazed with red-orange specks and mottling over transparent green, c. 1860-80. Height, Left 7¼", Right 6¼".

Ontario-German red earthenware pitchers, from southwestern Ontario, c. 1870. The left piece is brown-slip spattered over the red body, and the right piece over a yellow-green slip. Heights, Left 7⅝", Right 7".

*Pitcher and washbowl, decorated with floral motifs and rim
dashing of brown slip brushed over a base coating of white slip.
Western Ontario, mid to late 19th century, maker unknown.
Pitcher, height 12"; Bowl, diameter 11½".*

*Small redware pitcher, with hand impressed rather than coggled
bands, and a rough applied branch motif, lightly spattered with
brown slip, and a transparent but green-tinged glaze. Western
Ontario-German, c. 1860-70. Height 5¼".*

*Milk pitchers, both of white earthenware, with brown slip spatter,
decorated by spattering, and overglazed. Western Ontario, late
19th century. Height, Left 9½", Right 8⅝".*

Interior of the Ahrens Pottery at Paris, Ontario, c. 1880, with J. H. Ahrens mixing a glaze. From a painting in the collection of the Brant County Historical Society. The Ahrens Pottery was destroyed in a flood on the Grand River in 1883.

PARIS POTTERY.

PARIS, ONT., ______________ 188

M ______________

Bought of **J. H. AHRENS,**

POTTER.

Manufacturer of Flint Enamelled & Common Earthenware.

DOZ.		PER DOZ.	EACH.	$	CTS.
	Cream Pots.				
	6 Gallons........	7 20	0 60		
	4 "	4 80	0 40		
	2 "	3 00	0 25		
	1 "	1 50	0 12½		
	½ "	0 75	0 06¼		
	Milk Crocks.				
	2 Gallons........	2 40	0 20		
	1 "	1 50	0 12½		
	½ "	0 75	0 06¼		
	Milk Pans.				
	3 Gallons	3 00	0 25		
	2 "	2 25	0 18¾		
	1 "	1 50	0 12½		
	Butter Pots.				
	5 Gallons........	9 00	0 75		
	4 "	7 50	0 62½		
	3 "	6 00	0 50		
	2 "	4 50	0 37½		
	1 "	3 75	0 31¼		
	Jugs.				
	2 Gallons........	4 50	0 37½		
	1 "	3 00	0 25		
	½ "	2 25	0 18¾		
	¼ "	1 50	0 12½		
	Molasses Jugs.				
	1 Gallon........	3 00	0 25		
	½ "	2 25	0 18¾		
	¼ "	1 50	0 12½		
	Tomato, or Fruit Jars, with Corks				
	2 Gallons........	4 80	0 40		
	1 "	3 00	0 25		
	½ "	2 25	0 18¾		
	¼ "	1 50	0 12½		
	Preserve Jars with Covers				
	2 Gallons........	4 50	0 37½		
	1 "	3 00	0 25		
	½ "	2 25	0 18¾		
	¼ "	1 50	0 12½		
	Fancy Flower Pots.				
	1st Size........	4 50	0 37½		
	2nd "	3 00	0 25		

DOZ		PER DOZ.	EACH.	$	CTS.
	Water Pitchers.				
	1 Gallon........	3 00	0 25		
	½ "	2 25	0 18¾		
	¼ "	1 50	0 12½		
	Vases.				
	Per Pair........	4 50			
	Painted........	6 00			
	Stove Tubes.				
	1st Size........	3 00	0 25		
	2nd "	2 40	0 20		
	3rd "	1 80	0 15		
	Flower Pots.				
	12 Inch	3 60	0 30		
	10 "	2 40	0 20		
	8 "	1 50	0 12½		
	7 "	1 08	0 09		
	6 "	0 72	0 06		
	5 "	0 60	0 05		
	4 "	0 48	0 04		
	3 "	0 36	0 03		
	2½ "	0 18¾	0 01½		
	Saucers one-half the price of the Flower Pots.				
	ROCKINGHAM — OR — **Flint Enamelled Ware**				
	Water Pitchers.				
	1st Size........	7 50	0 62½		
	2nd "	4 50	0 37½		
	3rd "	3 00	0 25		
	4th "	2 25	0 18¾		
	6th "	1 50	0 12½		
	Tea Pots.				
	1st Size........	6 00	0 50		
	2nd "	4 50	0 37½		
	3rd "	3 00	0 25		
	Spittoons				
	1st Size........	7 50	0 62½		
	2nd "	6 00	0 50		
	3rd "	4 50	0 37½		
	4th "	3 00	0 25		
	5th "	2 40	0 20		
	Pie Plates.				
	1st Size........	0 96	0 08		
	2nd "	0 75	0 06¼		
	Hanging Flower Pots.				
	1st Size........	3 60	0 30		
	2nd "	2 40	0 20		

Price list and order forms of the J. H. Ahrens Pottery, Paris, about 1880. Most North American potteries of the later 19th century used handouts of this type, which served both as catalogues and as order forms.

Identical vases, one with white slip over buff earthenware, and the other brown slip coated. Both pieces are marked EBAN T GILBERT/PORT RYERSE (Ontario), and were made at the Marlatt-Gilbert Pottery, c. 1890. Heights 8½".

Spittoon and pitcher of white earthenware, and probably part of a larger set. Both pieces are coated in white slip, with an overlying violet spatter possibly done by adding a manganese glazing oxide to a brown slip. Both pieces are Ontario-Germanic, from Western Ontario, c. 1880-85, but the maker is unknown. Heights, Left 7", Right 10¼".

Buff earthenware pitcher and jug, attempts to simulate salt-glazed stoneware. Both pieces are coated with an off-white slip, decorated in copper green, and over-glazed. The pitcher is stamped under the decoration with an illegible maker's mark, but is from Western Ontario, c. 1870-80. The 2 gallon jug, c. 1865-67, is stamped JOSEPH WAGNER/POTTERY/BERLIN C.W. Heights, Left 10⅜", Right 13¼". Similar green-decorated white slip-coated wares were also made at the Burns Pottery, Markham, Ontario.

Covered redware jar, decorated with a sponging of green glaze mottled over a covering of yellow slip. Ontario-German, c. 1870-80. Height 9".

of two or three colours, oranges, greens, and yellows, depending on the glazing technique and firing conditions. The usual metallic oxide additives were iron, copper, or often both, with manganese or antimony used far less often. White tin glazes, or white slip coatings on pottery, were only rarely used by the Germanic potters. White finishes were much more in the English tradition, and only uncommonly encountered on Ontario pottery.

Hand-applied slip decorations, usually vestigial remnants of the elaborately decorated 18th century German and Pennsylvania-Germanic wares, were fairly common on 19th century Ontario-German pottery, but virtually unknown on pottery in the English or Anglo-American traditions. These decorations were usually done in brown slip applied by brush over the pottery body, dried, and then overglazed. Unlike both Pennsylvania and England, Ontario potters seem never to have used white slip for detail decorating of earthenware. Copper-green glazes, however, were occasionally spattered over a red clay body by Germanic potters. Green was likewise sometimes used over a buff-coloured body or slip, as brush-painted floral motifs, in an attempt to simulate the blue decorations on salt-glazed stoneware.

The shapes and forms of many earthenware pots were influenced by the container wares being produced by the salt-glazed stoneware industry, already dominant (and somewhat mechanized) by the time most Ontario potteries were established. Most small earthenware potters, working later in the century, seem to have started in business producing the latest of contemporary container shapes. They often then failed to change, ignoring or never becoming aware of shifts in design, and in some cases these potters continued making the same wares until well after 1900. Utility and container pottery, as the conservative Ontario earthenware makers produced it, shows little sign of having been much influenced by the vagaries of fashion or popular taste.

To offer just a couple of examples, the most common form of liquid storage jug in Ontario was cylindrical, with straight sides and convex shoulders rounding to the neck, essentially the same shape as a present-day glass gallon jug. This shape had been initiated for manufacturing ease by salt-glazed stoneware manufacturers about 1850, replacing an earlier but less stable bulbous-bodied and narrow-based form. Though the stoneware industry shifted in the 1890's to a machine-produced jug form, with straight-tapered or funnel-shaped shoulders, the earthenware producers never adopted the later type.

Typical Ontario open earthenware crocks or storage jars, like early jugs, had somewhat bulbous bodies, and rim diameters wider than bases. The stoneware industry switched in the 1860's to a more stable and more easily produced plain cylindrical crock type, a shape which, in spite of its simplicity, the Ontario earthenware potters never adopted. Bulbous-bodied crocks, almost everywhere else a form characteristic of the second quarter of the 19th century, were still the most common type coming out of Ontario earthenware potteries even after 1900.

The commercial earthenware producer in all areas of Canada was the victim of the rise of technology. The individual craft potter, turning his wares of a rough natural clay, already obsolescent as a ceramic material, by hand operations in a mechanical age, probably could not see that the craft as a whole in North America was in steep decline.

Census figures for Ontario show a steadily increasing number of active pottery establishments until 1880. The ratio between potteries and recorded numbers of working potters, however, never reached one to three. This indicated a proliferation of small craft shops rather than any growth of a factory system. In Quebec, where the earthenware business had never been strong, the opposite was occurring – ever fewer potteries employed growing numbers of potters.

Ontario in 1851 had approximately thirty potteries, and sixty-six people who listed their occupations as "potter". In 1861 there were some forty potteries and eighty-six potters. By 1871, 166 potters worked in fifty-eight potteries, and the census in 1881 recorded seventy-two potteries employing 182 potters. The decline, which was to accelerate rapidly, appeared first in the 1891 census, with figures which showed the number of potteries down to sixty, these employing 115 working potters.

The decline of the earthenware potters' craft, as of the whole commercial craft system, was of course quite irreversible. In Ontario, however, the rural earthenware potteries could survive, and even prosper, as long and only as long as their markets were isolated agricultural communities with relatively primitive environments and economies.

Typical Western Ontario-Germanic pudding and jelly moulds, glazed in a combination of copper-green and iron-red. Moulds of this type, c. 1860-90, were made by pressing a sheet of clay over a wooden or ceramic form. The rims were then probably finished and smoothed by wheel-turning. Diameters, Left 5⅛", Right 8¾".

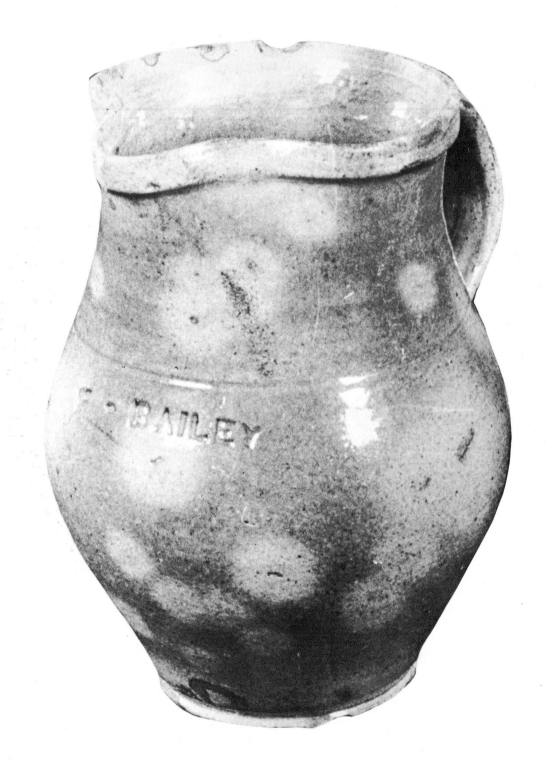

*Small red earthenware pitcher and jelly mould, the pitcher
stamped F. BAILEY in printer's type. No F. Bailey is known as a
potter, but he may have been a tavern-keeper or merchant who
ordered his name impressed on a quantity of pitchers. Both pieces
are glazed with iron-red spots over a transparent olive-green.
Ontario-German, pottery unknown, c. 1860-80. Heights, Left 6",
Right 4⅝".*

Dinner plates of red earthenware from the William Eby Pottery at Conestogo, Ontario, c. 1860-90. The Z shaped cherry stem was Eby's most common decorative motif, and the intact plate, upper right, is one of several known pieces. The rim-swagged plate in the centre and the sherds to the left, one with the tail of a whale, are unique. All pieces were decorated with brown slip applied by brush over biscuit pottery, and then lead overglazed. Diameters 8³/₄"-9¹/₂".

Large flowerpot with integral saucer, spattered with copper-green over a white slip. Ontario-German, probably from the Kitchener-Waterloo area, c. 1870. Diameter 8¾".

Red earthenware flowerpots with integral saucers, all Ontario-German and from western Ontario, c. 1860-80. The left piece is spattered with brown slip over the body; the large central and the right-hand pieces have a brown spattering over a coating of white-buff slip. Heights, Left 5¼", Centre 8", Right 6".

Covered jar of dense red earthenware, with applied handles and vine decoration. The piece is transparent glazed with an underlying fine brown spatter on the lid. Attributed to the George Taylor Pottery, Port Hope, Ontario, c. 1900-1915. Height (including lid) 14".

5 Earthenware of the Maritimes

The Maritime provinces of Canada — New Brunswick, Nova Scotia, Prince Edward Island and, for purposes of this book, Newfoundland — are the one area of Canada where the evident earliest production of pottery did not correspond to the period of early settlement. Likewise, the earthenware pottery of the Maritimes, in subtle ways, is quite distinctive and, unlike that of early Quebec or Ontario, is not apt to be confused with pottery of other areas. If met in a total vacuum — entirely without location or date context — it would be quite possible stylistically to interpret a pre-1850 Quebec piece as French, or most Ontario earthenware as northeastern United States, and the later moulded Rockingham and yellow-glazed wares as a basic type are, of course, North American Industrial. Except for the vague possibility of unknowledgeable confusion with a few English types, Maritimes pottery alone has sufficient unique characteristics to isolate it as a distinct category.

The Maritimes are an area of early settlement. French-speaking Acadians were settled along coastal areas of New Brunswick, Prince Edward Island, and Cape Breton Island (of Nova Scotia) by the late 17th century. The French had begun the huge fortified town of Louisbourg by 1715. The English had settled southern and western Nova Scotia by the first half of the 18th century; Halifax was founded in 1749. Yet none of these people are so far known to have produced even the roughest of earthenware. Living as they did along the coasts, all of the English and French inhabitants and settlements were so directly accessible to European supplies for virtually all their needs that native crafts had little chance.

As a result of this overseas dependence, there is no current evidence that any native potteries developed much before the early 19th century, fully 200 years after first settlement. The French at Louisbourg had a brick-yard and kiln at Mira Gut, some ten miles north, in the early 18th century, and extremely rough and heavy earthenware sherds recovered at Louisbourg suggest the possibility of local pottery production, but as yet there is no real evidence of this, and the Mira site has not been examined.

I would suspect that there were probably a very

few potteries in the Maritimes by the late 18th century, though there is no real documentary confirmation. A Samuel Marshall listed his occupation as "potter" in tax assessment rolls at Blue Hill, Nova Scotia, in 1786-87, but this alone does not necessarily mean that he was in fact operating a pottery.

The earliest confirmed commercial potter in the Maritimes appears to have been John Thomas, at Portland, New Brunswick, who was in business and advertising by 1814. Then James Ellis, at Dipper Harbour, New Brunswick, operated a pottery for about ten years in the 1830's and '40's, making ordinary containers and utility pieces. Matthew Thompson established a pottery a bit later, about 1848, at St. John, New Brunswick, the Thompson Pottery operating into the 1880's.

With only the single exception of the White-Foley pottery at St. John, New Brunswick, all Maritimes pottery consisted of dense red-earthenware container and utility wares. The most common types presently found are milk bowls, stoppered jugs, pitchers, and covered jars, probably indicative of the range and balance of original production. Tablewares, however, the forms most generally imported, are rarely found as products of local potteries. Thus it seems that, while the Maritimes potters perhaps produced a somewhat greater range than the potters of early Quebec, they could not economically produce nearly as great a variety of wares as the Ontario earthenware industry.

Most of the later 19th century potters in the Maritimes, and there was no great number of them, were English in origin and training. This appears as a very strong influence on their pottery, though the equally definite influence of environment and economy also makes this pottery very much a North American type.

The earthenware of the Maritimes shows a characteristically English heavy use of white tin glazes, or white slips under glaze. Thus milk bowls, made in all sizes, are typically coated completely with white slip or glaze on the interiors, while exteriors are left unglazed. Covered jars and crocks are likewise often lined with white, and pitchers, though perhaps less often, still commonly so.

Newspaper advertisement of John Thomas, Portland, N.B., of 1814-15.

Large red earthenware utility bowl, with a crudely trailed
decoration in white slip under a transparent glaze. The sherds in
foreground are from the Prince Edward Island Pottery, 1880-95,
Charlottetown, P.E.I., where numerous reconstructable bowls of
this type were recovered during the 1970 excavations.
Diameter 12½".

Though English earthenware makers of the 19th century also made great use of white tin glazes or ball-clay slip, as it was called, they did not use it for complete vessel linings in the Maritimes manner. Neither did the rest of Canada, or earthenware potters in the United States; exterior white slip coatings on red-earthenware are most uncommon in these areas, and white linings quite rare.

For glazing the outer surfaces of jars, jugs, and pitchers, the Maritimes potters generally used the same basic lead glaze, sometimes with light colouring additives, as did all earthenware potters everywhere. The standard technique was to hold the pot being glazed by its sides at the base, and to dip it, open end down, into a tub of glaze mixture. This would coat both rim and sides, but not the interior.

In doing this, however, the Maritimes potter dipped only to within an inch or two of the base of each vessel, avoided getting his fingers wet, and consequently left the lowest exterior part of each piece unglazed. This same characteristic I have often noticed on rough English earthenware. The Ontario-German potter, conversely, dipped his pots fully to the base in glaze, often leaving finger marks showing where he had held the piece.

Occasionally, too, Maritimes potters used white slip purely for decorative lines and motifs, again in the English (and by derivation, American) manner. This, again, is virtually unknown on other Canadian pottery; the Quebecois did no line slip decorating, and the Ontario potters used brown or green. Perhaps the best examples of white slip applied as decoration, and of its rudimentary nature compared to the English, are the Prince Edward Island Pottery bowls with wide loops of white slip on their interiors, under lead glaze. We recovered and reconstructed numbers of these from excavations in 1970, though the same pottery, established around 1880, also produced even greater quantities of plain white-lined milk bowls. All of these wares were shipped throughout the Maritimes, a much wider than usual distribution for earthenware.

Charlottetown, Prince Edward Island, had had an earlier Spring Park Pottery, opened in 1864

Three typical Maritimes pieces, two pitchers and an open crock. All three pieces are of a very dark red earthenware, the interiors lined with a white slip, and the exteriors covered, except for the base portions, with a transparent glaze. Nova Scotia or Prince Edward Island, c. 1870-80. Heights, Left 9⅛", Centre 10¼", Right 9½".

and closed about 1885. The later Prince Edward Island Pottery was managed by Frank Hornsby, who before coming to Charlottetown had worked in his father's pottery and brickworks at Dartmouth, Nova Scotia. In the period of the 1860's to '90's, several earthenware potteries operated around Halifax and Enfield, Nova Scotia, and St. John, New Brunswick, because of the proximity of good clay. Except, however, for the wares of the Prince Edward Island Pottery and of the White-Foley Pottery at St. John, it is not yet really possible to make direct attributions of pieces found today to their exact origins. Most of this pottery, other than special examples, as elsewhere is not marked.

The largest and most important pottery in the Maritimes was that of Joseph White, who in 1861 left his pottery factory in Bristol, England, for St. John, New Brunswick, and produced not earthenware but stoneware, finished with white ball-slip rather than salt-glaze, as was then becoming standard in England. Importing clay from New Jersey, the White Pottery manufactured hand-turned utility wares and jars, characterized by white exterior finishes, and often with brown slip interior linings. The White Pottery wares are unmarked, and apparently the only moulded slip-cast pieces produced were simple pitchers. In the 1880's Joseph White's grandson, James Foley, took over the factory in a partnership with Samuel Poole that lasted until 1898, after which Fenwick Foley, James' son, operated until the factory became Foley Potteries, Ltd., in 1921. The company's successor is now Canuck Pottery, Ltd., at Labelle, Quebec — the only firm other than the Campbell Pottery at Hamilton, Ontario, that has managed to adapt, and change materials, technology, products and markets, to continue to the present day.

The Maritimes earthenware potteries, like those of Quebec, were always tenuous operations in direct competition with inexpensive importations, and none are known to have survived after 1900. Though they turned out only a quite limited range of very simple utility ware, with only occasional urges toward experimentation or special pieces, the pottery of the Maritimes is of rather special interest because of the mixture of characteristics which make it a type unique to its own area.

Covered jar, red-buff earthenware with two white bands circling both jar and cover. The lead glaze extends to within an inch of the base. Probably Nova Scotia, c. 1850-80. Height 8¼".

Nova Scotia small storage jars. In the Maritimes fashion, all have the lower part of the outside left unglazed. The two outside pieces are finished with a dark manganese-in-lead glaze; the centre pieces are transparent-glazed. Nova Scotia, c. 1870-90. Heights, Left to Right, 6½", 7½", 6½", 7⅝".

Large Nova Scotia storage crock, with four lug handles, and decorated with two bands of white slip. These pieces are typically found in Nova Scotia, c. 1860-90, but the pottery which produced them is presently unknown. Height 14¹/₄".

2 gallon earthenware jug, lead glazed with orange mottling, and marked P.E.I./POTTERY. More elaborate than most, this jug has the coggled decoration typical of this pottery, c. 1880-90. Height 12¹/₂".

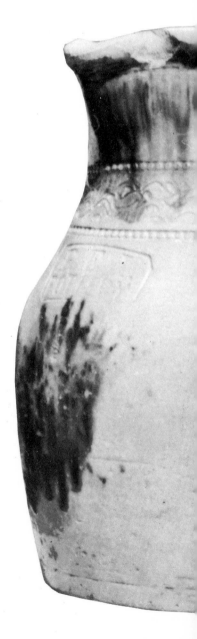

Three earthenware pitchers, with transparent green-tinged glazes over spattering and sponging in brown slip. All of the pieces have the characteristic coggled decoration of the Prince Edward Island Pottery, and two of the three pieces are marked P.E.I./POTTERY. Heights, Left to Right 7³/₄", 8³/₄", 7³/₈".

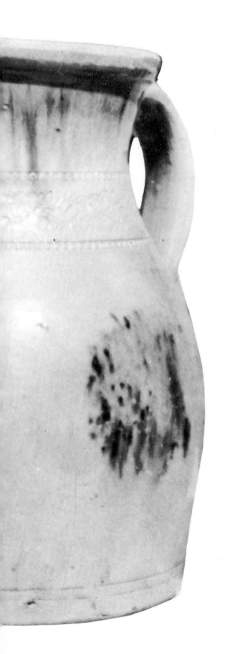

Red earthenware cake storage crock, unmarked but with coggled decoration typical of the P.E.I. Pottery. The applied letters spelling CAKE are formed of white pipe clay. Prince Edward Island Pottery, Charlottetown, c. 1890-1900. Diameter 10³/₄".

Red earthenware tobacco jar and matched cup, made from separately moulded and assembled pieces, and Rockingham-glazed. This elaborate piece, dating from the 1890's, is marked P.E.I./POTTERY. Unfinished components of these tobacco and pipe sets were found in the excavations of the pottery. Length 10¼".

Stoneware pitcher, brown-slip lined, and with white tin-oxide glaze. The piece is decorated with a swagged band in blue glaze. White-Foley Pottery, St. John, N.B., c. 1870-1890. Heights 9".

Three English stoneware jugs, of types imported in great quantity during the 19th century, and all stamped with Maritimes merchant's marks. The left piece, salt-glazed over a white slip, is marked "JAS. C. BAIRD/ST. JOHNS, NFLD". The centre piece, salt-glazed over brown slip, is marked simply "VATES", and the right hand jug carries a separately applied clay label stamped "I. S. ARENSON & CO./PICTOU/NOVA SCOTIA". All three pieces date c. 1860-1880. Heights, Left 12¼", Centre 12½", Right 10½".

6 Miniatures, Toys and Whimseys

Perhaps the most unusual pottery made in Canada, and coming to be among the scarcest, was the one type that does not fit into any of the usual utilitarian categories—miniatures and toys, decorative whimseys, and later saleman's samples. Pieces such as these occurred in a great variety of forms, from copies of larger vessels to moulded figures, and they stimulate a great deal of collector interest not only because of size, but because of a quality of uniqueness and the obvious special care and attention that went into making them.

Miniatures can basically be divided into two groups—the hand-formed pieces and the cast or moulded types. The former are largely of red earthenware, usually unique, and products of the small craft potteries. Some toys and most of the salesman's samples were hand turned or slip-cast in moulds of a high firing earthenware or stoneware, though produced in very small quantity.

The making of unique miniatures and small special pieces was a particular avocation of the Germanic potters, and in Canada such pottery occurs almost exclusively in southwestern Ontario. The hand-made miniatures, particularly, represent virtually the only really individual artistic endeavours of the potters other than rare large special-order pieces. As such, the miniatures offer an insight into the Ontario-German pottery that one would never get from standard production wares.

The Germanic potters, perhaps more than any other group in North America, often used their clay to express themselves and their culture, as well as to make their tenuous living. The clay was a medium many of them obviously loved and had a special feel for, beyond the confines of bread-and-butter manufactures. Many earthenware miniatures were made simply for personal enjoyment—often as gifts to children or friends, sometimes as tests of skill and materials, occasionally as pure experimentation, and sometimes probably for no overt reason. These unique and special little pieces, however, most clearly represent the aesthetic side of the earthenware potters' craft, even given the diminishing Germanic tradition.

The making of toys and miniatures had also long been a habit of Pennsylvania-German potters,

Salt-glazed stoneware jugs, with incised initials "A.B." and "A.B. JR.", probably of the recipients of these pieces as gifts. Hart Pottery, Picton, Ontario, c. 1870. Heights 3½".

Moulded stoneware toy or doll house chest of drawers, with a wood-coloured brown Rockingham glaze. The piece is unmarked but probably from the Brantford Pottery, c. 1870-90. Height 3".

Saleman's sample salt-glazed stoneware container, very carefully made, and marked with a Brantford Pottery stamp. The jar is probably from the Goold period at Brantford, c. 1860-67. Height, 3⅝".

who as early as the mid 18th century had produced small pieces ranging from little crocks and jars to elaborate moulded or sculpted birds, often as clay whistles. In the 19th century, though the quality of work declined with the whole level of Pennsylvania decorative arts, miniatures continued to be made in great quantity, often finished with almost garishly coloured glazes. The best known of such pieces are perhaps the vast variety of products of the Bell Potteries at Strasburg, Virginia, and Waynesboro, Pennsylvania. These later 19th century types were often almost identical with the forms made by Germanic potters in Ontario during the same period.

Known Ontario makers include men such as Daniel Orth at Campden, John Kulp of Grimsby, William Eby at Conestogo, J. H. Ahrens of Paris, and Adam Bierenstahl of Bridgeport. There were certainly many others. In Ontario their influence also spread to area stoneware factories, most notably the Hart Pottery at Picton and the Brantford Pottery. Both factories had workmen, perhaps themselves trained in the Germanic tradition, who on occasion made salt-glazed stoneware miniatures.

Ontario potters never produced miniatures in the quantities of the German areas of the U.S., and these little pieces have become most uncommon and highly sought as a result. There is also no evidence, or any single example that I know of, of the making of red earthenware miniatures anywhere else in Canada, either by the Quebecois potters or the English potters of the Maritimes.

As well as the unique miniature and toy earthenware pieces of the Ontario German potters, the larger factories also made limited numbers of tiny salesman's samples – miniature crocks and jugs small enough for packing in a suitcase, all exact replicas of full-sized production wares, and very carefully fashioned and finished to attract orders. Only the larger companies which employed salesmen, of course, produced such pieces, and those known from the Brantford Pottery seem to be the most varied. However, factories such as Cap Rouge, Farrar, and Robert Campbell/Canada Potteries, may have made such samples occasionally as well.

In the late 19th century, by far the most popular of purely decorative non-utilitarian pottery, or

Ontario-German red-earthenware coin bank, an unusually elaborate piece covered with moulded figures of doves, attributed to the Samuel Burns Pottery, Markham, Ontario, c. 1875. The piece is spattered in brown slip, over-glazed, and in style is very similar to Pennsylvania-German pieces of the same and earlier periods. Height 5½".

Pair of red earthenware moulded dog figures, or King Charles Spaniels, brown slip spattered and over-glazed, made at the John Brown Pottery, Bowmanville, Ontario, c. 1855. Height 14".

Red earthenware moulded dogs, western Ontario, both brown slip spattered and over-glazed. The left piece is slotted in the head as a coin bank, and is unmarked. The finer right-hand piece is incised in the base "Nov 11, 1861", a mark without present meaning. The makers are unknown. Heights, Left 9¼", Right 9½".

whimseys, were moulded dog figures—the King Charles Spaniels, so-called from the dogs Charles II brought from France at the Restoration in 1660. Similar seated-dog figures were manufactured in vast quantities, of white earthenware and ironstone, by the Staffordshire potteries, and heavily imported into Canada. The King Charles Spaniels were so popular, however, that even the Ontario red-earthenware producers spotted a chance to compete. From the number and variety of these figures existing today, it would seem that every potter with any knowledge or capability at all of slip-casting produced them at one time or another. Known makers include not only Brantford and the Hart Pottery at Picton, but also earthenware producers such as John Kulp, Samuel Burns at Markham, John Brown at Bowmanville, who even patented his design, as well as several Waterloo County potters, all people who are not known to have ever produced any other slip-cast wares. The height of popularity of earthenware King Charles Spaniels seemed to be from about 1885 to 1880—few are found to be datable later than that.

Finally, a fourth category of unusual forms comprised the specially-made utility pieces, pottery objects not quite small enough to be called miniatures, but which had definite purposes—coin banks, egg cups, salt cellars, small jugs, jars, and bowls, serving kegs (probably for cider), and myriad other forms. Pieces such as these—the sort of thing potters might make as individual gifts for friends, were again certainly most commonly fabricated at the Germanic earthenware potteries, but they are not unknown from the stoneware and Rockingham factories.

Except for salesmans' samples, exercises of individual talent and motivation—unique toys, whimseys, and unusual gift pieces—rather died out as the ceramics factories became dominant and the earthenware craft potteries disappeared. In the 20th century there was no longer much time for that sort of thing nor, with the ceramic worker increasingly an industrial employee rather than a craftsman, much of any opportunity or desire.

Miniature crock and small covered bowl, both excavated at the William Eby Pottery, Conestogo, Ontario. The miniature crock has brown slip brushed on over a red pottery body. The bowl is decorated with dark brown, red-brown, and yellowish slip spatter. Both pieces are overglazed. c. 1860-80. Heights, Left 1½", Right 2⅝".

Small redware platter, coated with yellow-buff slip, brown slip spattered, and finally over-glazed. The piece was probably pressed from a slab of clay in an open mould, and has a pattern in relief of Diana the Huntress in the centre. Southwestern Ontario, Germanic influence, c. 1870-80. Length 7".

Miniature barrel, with closed ends, and bung and spigot holes. The raised banding is painted and the incised stave joints filled with brown slip, also used for the date inscription "R.1862", all underglaze. Probably a bar-top serving cask, the piece was possibly made by Abraham Roszel of Grimsby, Ontario. Height 9".

Miniature stoneware pitchers and jardinieres, probably salesman's samples, glazed in mottled browns, blues, and greens. Brantford Pottery, Brantford, Ontario, c. 1885-94. Heights, Left to Right 1⁵/₈", ⁷/₈", 1", 1¹/₂".

Small covered salt cellar or sugar bowl, densely green-glazed but with an under-lying iron oxide spatter. Made at the William Eby Pottery, Conestogo, c. 1885-90. Diameter 4⁷/₈".

7 Salt-glazed Stoneware

Stoneware is a hard and durable pottery, still technically an earthenware since the clay occurs naturally, but a material far superior to red earthenware. It is not easily chipped or broken and, being structurally strong, is suitable for considerably finer and lighter wares than it was typically used for in Canada.

Clay for stoneware contains a relatively high silica content, and the pottery must be fired at a higher temperature, 2000 to 2200 degrees Farenheit, than redware. This fuses the silica, and results in a vitrified body which is non-porous even without a covering glaze.

Stoneware and semi-porcelain were developed in China well before 1000 A.D., and Arab caravans were trading them to Europe by late medieval times. German potters who had discovered the Chinese materials and methods were producing stoneware by the 13th century. Rather than copying Chinese coloured glazes, however, the Germans developed, perhaps after accidental discovery, a technique of salt-glazing whereby common salt, vaporized in the extreme heat of the pottery-firing kiln, combined chemically with the silica in the body of the pottery to form a transparent sodium silicate glaze. Produced continually in Germany, and later in England, salt-glazed stoneware for several centuries remained the strongest and most satisfactory known ceramic material, until in the late 18th century it was replaced for finer wares by semi-china clays.

Stoneware production was late in coming to Canada, and not until 1840 or 1841 was the first pottery established, at St. Johns, Quebec. The causes for the delayed establishment of potteries were twofold. First, there was then no known source of suitable stoneware clay available anywhere in Canada. Throughout the Northeast, American stoneware since the 1770's had been made from clay mined at Amboy, New Jersey, and shipped from there to various potteries by sloop or barge. The same material was used by all Canadian stoneware potteries, the clay brought from New Jersey via the Hudson River, the Erie Canal, the Great Lakes, and Lake Champlain, and in Canada, the Richelieu, St. Lawrence, and Grand Rivers. All stoneware potteries were thus necessarily located, above all, for direct navigable water access. This was also of great benefit in shipping out finished pottery to distant parts.

Since there was no established stoneware or factory-system pottery industry in Canada before the mid 19th century, there were no people both trained in the business and possessing the capital to set up potteries. Considering also the problems of clay importation, of building high-temperature kilns, and the costs and complexity of the machinery and moulds required for manufacturing anything other than hand-formed container wares, setting up a stoneware factory was quite a different proposition from starting a rural earthenware pottery.

The great majority of the stoneware made in Canada was in the class of heavy salt-glazed containers—jugs, crocks, jars, bowls, and so on; wares of this type still comprised the bulk of the market. Stoneware containers, to be sure, were superior to competitive red earthenware, but they were also somewhat more expensive. Because of the qualities of stoneware the demand was continuous, but prices increased steadily with time. This may have at least contributed to the decline and eventual disappearance of salt-glazed stoneware, as it came into competition with mass produced and cheap glass late in the century.

The potter-entrepreneurs who set up the original stoneware potteries were Americans, importing their talents and capital, and all had long experience in the industry. Samuel Hart, who started the Hart Pottery at Picton in 1849, was a member of a family which, singly and collectively, had operated potteries at Fulton, Sherburne, and Ogdensburg, New York, for nearly twenty years. Justin Morton, who established at Brantford the same year, came from several years at the Clark Pottery at Lyons, New York. Moses Farrar, who set up business at St. Johns, Quebec, about 1840, was of a family which also operated a stoneware pottery at Fairfax, Vermont, with another branch of the family manufacturing stoneware at Geddes (Syracuse), New York.

Given this beginning, the salt-glazed containers and later moulded wares produced by the Canadian stoneware industry were logically derived from American types—identical forms and shapes produced by the same methods and

Early salt-glazed stoneware pieces, dating from the 1840's or
'50's. At left is a dark pitcher, found in Nova Scotia and decorated
in blue with a flower design and a trailed zig-zag line around the
neck. Probably of New England origin. The crock on the right, of
an early shape, is decorated with a simple floral motif in blue, and
is marked MANUFACTURED FOR/R. MCPAUL & CO./
PICTON, CW. The piece is probably an early product of the Hart
Pottery at Picton, Ontario, c. 1850-55, though the shape is also
suggestive of upper New York State. Heights, Left 11³/₄", 8⁷/₈".

techniques. There does not seem to have been much English influence on the Canadian stoneware industry, and what little is evident appears limited to secondary influences, through American pottery or the copying of a few imported forms. In the existing scheme a British potter-entrepreneur could probably do better at home, producing whitewares for export.

Stoneware vessels were made much as any other pottery—hand-formed with the aid of a few rim-shaping ribs and size gauges. Once air-dried, the pottery was then very often decorated with designs or pictures, always with a cobalt oxide glaze which fired to a rich blue, the only inexpensive colouring oxide which matured at stoneware firing temperatures. These blue decorations ran the gamut from simple floral motifs to birds and animals, and even scenes which included ships, houses, and figures. They were always hand-applied, either with a brush or a slip-cup quill, described earlier, and the better decorations often showed considerable imagination and complexity, if not necessarily artistic talent.

This hand-decorating of salt-glazed stoneware seems to have been a peculiarly American practice, and from it Canadian, which began in the late 18th century. Early German grey stonewares, types from which the North American are derived, were often decorated using cobalt blue, usually with geometric or moulded relief motifs, but never with painted or incised pictures.

Once decorated (though far from all pieces were) the pottery was ready for firing, usually in huge wood or charcoal heated kilns, in a firing operation which took four to eight days. Once the kiln was loaded and the fires started, the temperature was raised, maintained, and then slowly dropped as in firing earthenware, but over a longer time period. At maximum temperature the glazing operation took place.

When the pottery had been heated to about 2200 degrees, after perhaps a day of firing, a vent was removed from the kiln and, avoiding the searing heat, a man shovelled in common rock salt, sometimes as much as a bushel. Each shovel-load of salt, on hitting the heat of the kiln interior, vaporized into component gasses, sodium and chlorine. The gaseous sodium, vaporized from the salt, then chemically combined with the silica in the pottery (and all other exposed surfaces) to create the hard and impermeable surface coating of sodium silicate glaze, a form of glass.

The resulting salt-glaze, as it was called, was quite superior to the lead glaze of earthenware, for it was a part of the body of the pottery rather than a separate (and flakeable) layer. It was also, unlike earthenware lead glaze, insoluble in water and non-toxic. Transparent and showing the buff or grey body colour of the clay, salt-glazing was restricted to the exteriors of stoneware pottery. The reason for this was simply that salt-glazing, applied as a gas rather than a liquid, did not evenly or reliably penetrate to or coat the interiors of some vessels, particularly narrow necked jugs. Thus as early as 1800 American stoneware makers had begun lining the insides of nearly all container wares with a high-firing and siliceous brown slip, as a liquid which could be washed around to coat every surface and corner. All Canadian salt-glazed pottery was brown slip lined in the same manner, and smaller pieces often were entirely slip-coated, rather than salt-glazed.

There were never many stoneware producers in Canada at any time, probably again because of a small population and market, and the problems and costs of importing the clay and most other components. Among the stoneware factories, however, the more major producers operated for quite long periods, in spite of changing markets, economic depressions, and often disastrous fires.

The earliest stoneware potters in Canada were the Farrars of Vermont, Moses and Ebenezer, who established a factory at St. Johns, Quebec, apparently about 1840. They also operated a pottery only sixty-five miles away, at Fairfax, Vermont, which simplified their logistics and the shipment of clay supplies. The St. Johns factory was a partnership, Farrar and Soule, for a few years in the 1850's, burned and was rebuilt in 1857, and on the death of Ebenezer Farrar that year was taken over by his younger brother, George Whitefield Farrar. The pottery again burned in 1876, and was rebuilt at Iberville, across the Richelieu River. When George Whitefield Farrar died in 1881, Ebenezer's son

6 gallon salt-glazed crock, decorated in slip-trailed blue glaze with two standing birds. The crock is stamped S. SKINNER & CO./PICTON, C.W., c. 1864-67. Height 14½".

3 gallon jardiniere, c. 1870, with very unusual applied handles of moulded faces of dogs. The piece is marked G.I. LAZIER, PICTON, C.W. Height 8⅝".

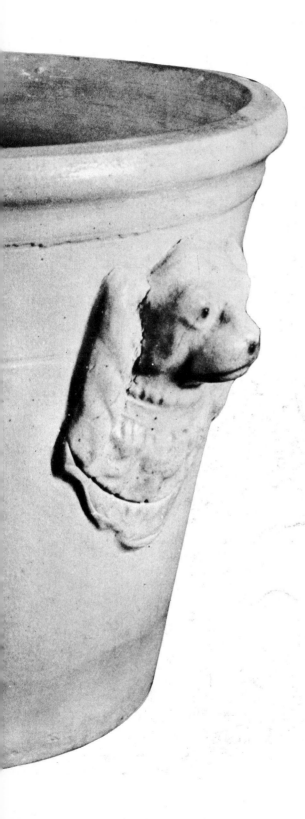

George H. assumed control, and ran the business until his own death in 1927. Only then, long after the height of popularity of salt-glazed stoneware, and the demise of every other stoneware pottery in Canada, did the Farrar Pottery finally close.

Two other stoneware makers operated for only a short time in St. Johns. Orrin Ballard, who also had a pottery in Burlington, Vermont, produced salt-glaze during the late 1850's, then after 1860 relocated in Cornwall, Ontario, and by 1866 was back in Burlington. John Gillespie operated the Canada Stoneware Manufacturing Establishment at St. Johns from 1853 to about 1863, when that pottery closed.

Samuel Hart in 1849 began one of the two initial stoneware potteries in Upper Canada, at Picton on Lake Ontario, and ran it until 1855, when his uncle, Samuel Skinner, took over as manager. In 1867 a Hart son-in-law, George Lazier, assumed management of the factory in Picton until his death in 1887. A new company, Hart Brothers & Lazier, had been formed in Belleville in 1880; after Lazier's death in 1887 the Picton factory was closed, with all production concentrated at the new Belleville Pottery. Charles Hart, and after 1910 his nephew Robert, managed Hart Brothers & Lazier, the market ever declining, until the company was finally sold about 1925 and ceased operation.

Also in 1849, Justin Morton came to Brantford, Ontario, from Lyons, New York, and started a small stoneware business, evidently with the help of some local capital. After two partnerships, and then leasing the pottery for a year, a Brantford businessman and Morton partner, Franklin P. Goold, bought the pottery and managed it until 1867. As well as salt-glazed stoneware, both Morton and Goold had experimented with moulded hollow-wares and ceramic picture frames, a few of which are known, but production of these forms was never extensive.

Goold in 1867 sold the business to a partnership of William E. Welding, his plant manager, and William Belding. The factory burned in 1873, and Welding bought out his partner and rebuilt, to operate as sole owner until 1894. The pottery burned a second time in 1883, and was again rebuilt on the same site. In 1884 Henry Schuler came as plant manager, having lost his own stoneware pottery at Paris, Ontario, in a flood in 1883. Schuler exercised a great change in the product line, though salt-glazed containers continued as the mainstay of the business. Finally, in 1894, Welding retired and sold the pottery, which was reorganized as a joint-stock company, the Brantford Stoneware Manufacturing Company, with Schuler as Secretary and Plant Manager. The company was finally dissolved, the building sold, and production ceased in 1907. The Brantford Pottery site was excavated in 1967.

Most of the larger and longer-lived stoneware potteries, such as the Farrar establishment, Brantford, and Picton-Belleville, diversified manufactures in the 1870's and '80's to moulded and slip-cast tablewares (see chapter 8). Though salt-glazed containers were never entirely given up, it was certainly this spreading-out of production, to fill markets much larger than that for container wares alone, that allowed these potteries to survive as long as they did.

A few other salt-glazed factories operated from the 1860's to shortly after 1900, all of lesser importance and shorter-lived. At Cornwall, Ontario, Flack and Van Arsdale established the Cornwall Pottery about 1868, the business continuing until about 1910 in spite of production of containers alone. Two small container factories existed in Toronto, the Don Bridge Pottery of Warner & Co. in the late 1850's and of Nicholas Eberhardt in the 1860's and '70's, and the Toronto Stoneware Pottery of James R. Burns in the 1880's. Some factories were even set up to manufacture only a limited range of specialized stoneware containers, such as the Glass Brothers of London, Ontario, who in the late 1800's and '90's emphasized production of sealer jars for home canning.

In general, however, it was extremely difficult for any of these pottery factories to prosper, and ultimately to survive, limited as they were first to container production for an ever-declining home food preservation market, and to a basic dependence on the vagaries and variations of naturally-occuring clays. The stoneware factories, and the first generation of the Canadian ceramics industry, thus eventually disappeared. It was to be replaced gradually, of course, in the 20th century by a second-generation and wholly modern industry, which, as today, depends on standardized white china clays and, through these materials, standardization of technology and equipment.

Jug and hot-water bottle, both decorated with birds in trailed blue glaze, that on the left more like a sea serpent. Both pieces are marked G.I. LAZIER, the operator of the Hart Pottery in Picton, Ontario, in the 1870's. Height, Left 9³⁄₄", Length, Right 10¹⁄₂".

Advertisements of the Hart Brothers & Lazier pottery at Belleville,
Ontario; above from the Ontario Directory *for 1882, centre from*
the Ontario Provincial Directory *of 1884-5, and below from the*
. . . Directory for 1886.

HART BROS. & LAZIER,

MANUFACTURERS OF

WATER FILTERS,

ALSO

STONEWARE

OF EVERY DESCRIPTION.

All goods made from the best Imported Clay.   Write for Prices.

BELLEVILLE, ONT.

Beaverton, Ont.,

M *Joseph Downer* — *Onlon* — 1895

Bought of R. McCALLUM,

—MANUFACTURER OF—

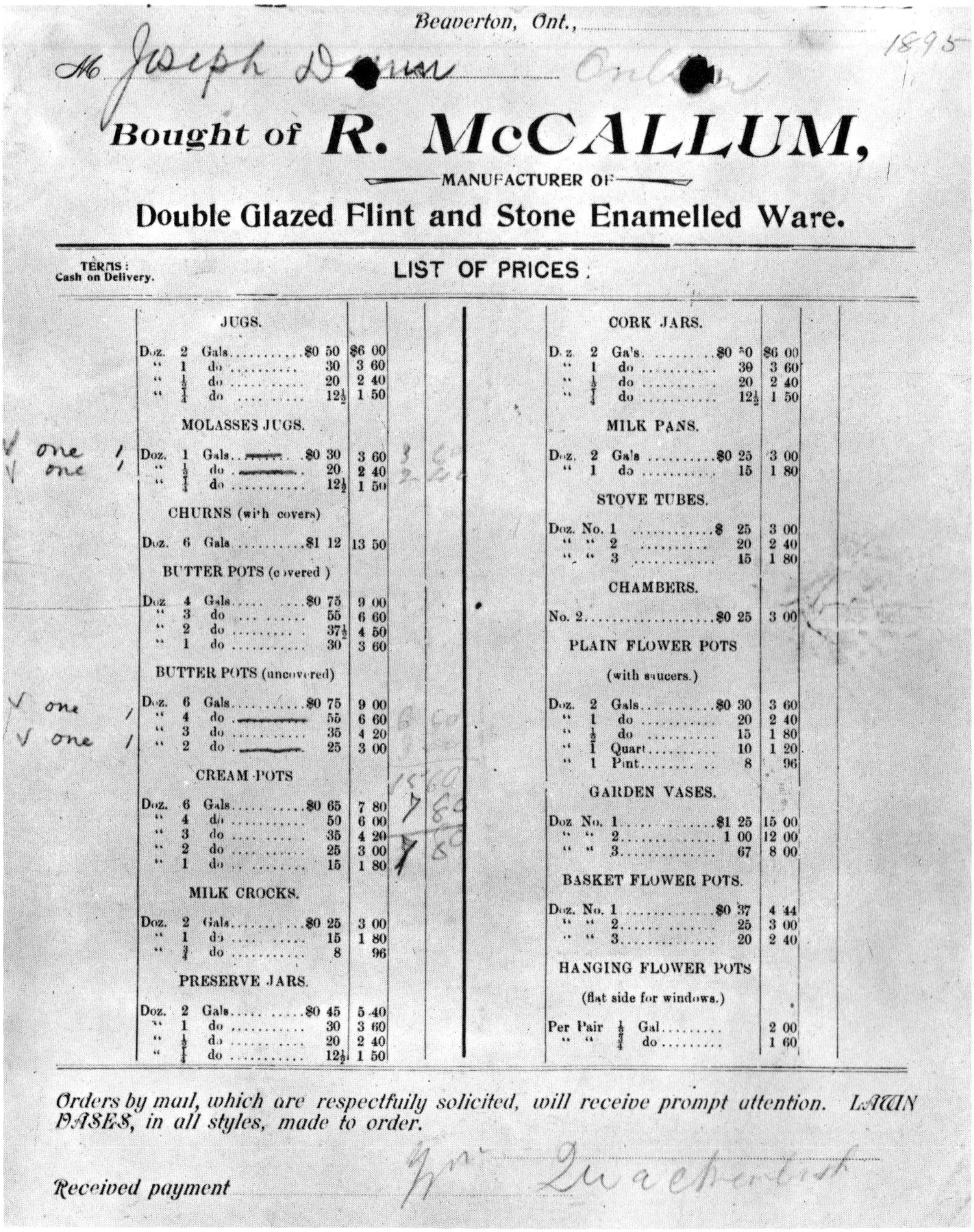

Double Glazed Flint and Stone Enamelled Ware.

TERMS:
Cash on Delivery.

LIST OF PRICES.

JUGS.		
Doz. 2 Gals..........$0 50	$6 00
" 1 do 30	3 60
" ½ do 20	2 40
" ¼ do 12½	1 50

MOLASSES JUGS.		
Doz. 1 Gals..........$0 30	3 60
" ½ do 20	2 40
" ¼ do 12½	1 50

✓ one /
✓ one /

CHURNS (with covers)		
Doz. 6 Gals..........$1 12	13 50

BUTTER POTS (covered)		
Doz. 4 Gals..........$0 75	9 00
" 3 do 55	6 60
" 2 do 37½	4 50
" 1 do 30	3 60

BUTTER POTS (uncovered)		
Doz. 6 Gals..........$0 75	9 00
" 4 do 55	6 60
" 3 do 35	4 20
" 2 do 25	3 00

✓ one /
✓ one /

CREAM POTS		
Doz. 6 Gals..........$0 65	7 80
" 4 do 50	6 00
" 3 do 35	4 20
" 2 do 25	3 00
" 1 do 15	1 80

MILK CROCKS.		
Doz. 2 Gals..........$0 25	3 00
" 1 do 15	1 80
" ¾ do 8	96

PRESERVE JARS.		
Doz. 2 Gals..........$0 45	5 40
" 1 do 30	3 60
" ½ do 20	2 40
" ¼ do 12½	1 50

CORK JARS.		
Doz. 2 Ga's..........$0 50	$6 00
" 1 do 30	3 60
" ½ do 20	2 40
" ¼ do 12½	1 50

MILK PANS.		
Doz. 2 Gals..........$0 25	3 00
" 1 do 15	1 80

STOVE TUBES.		
Doz. No. 1 ....$ 25	3 00
" " 2 20	2 40
" " 3 15	1 80

CHAMBERS.		
No. 2..........$0 25	3 00

PLAIN FLOWER POTS		
(with saucers.)		
Doz. 2 Gals..........$0 30	3 60
" 1 do 20	2 40
" ½ do 15	1 80
" 1 Quart 10	1 20
" 1 Pint.......... 8	96

GARDEN VASES.		
Doz No. 1 ....$1 25	15 00
" " 2.......... 1 00	12 00
" " 3.......... 67	8 00

BASKET FLOWER POTS.		
Doz. No. 1 ....$0 37	4 44
" " 2 25	3 00
" " 3.......... 20	2 40

HANGING FLOWER POTS		
(flat side for windows.)		
Per Pair ½ Gal.........	2 00
" " ¼ do	1 60

Orders by mail, which are respectfully solicited, will receive prompt attention. LAWN VASES, *in all styles, made to order.*

Received payment — *Wm Quackenbush*

The Cap Rouge Pottery, Cap Rouge, P.Q., about 1885, from an early photograph. The Pottery and its kilns had been demolished by 1900.

The Brantford Pottery — Brantford Stoneware Manufacturing Co., in 1895. This was the third pottery building, built in 1883 and finally demolished in 1966.

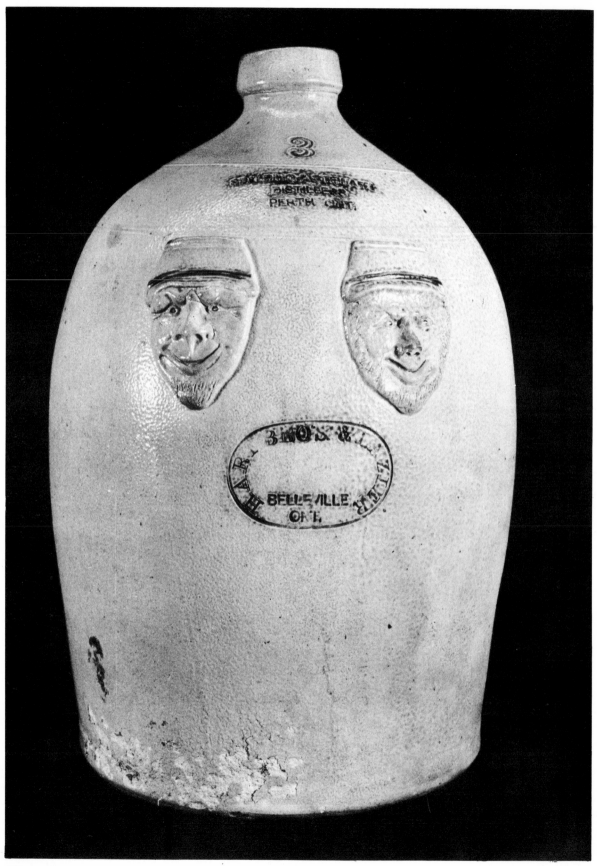

3 gallon jug, decorated with two impressed toby masks filled with blue glaze, c. 1880-90. The jug is marked above the masks SPALDING & STEWART/DISTILLERS/PERTH, ONT., and the maker's mark below, HART BROS. & LAZIER/BELLEVILLE/ONT. Height 15½".

Baking casserole, decorated with crudely brushed blue floral motifs, and marked FROM/S. ROGERS/THE CHEAPEST STORE/IN BATH (Ont.). Probably from the Hart Pottery, Picton or Belleville, c. 1870-90. Diameter 12".

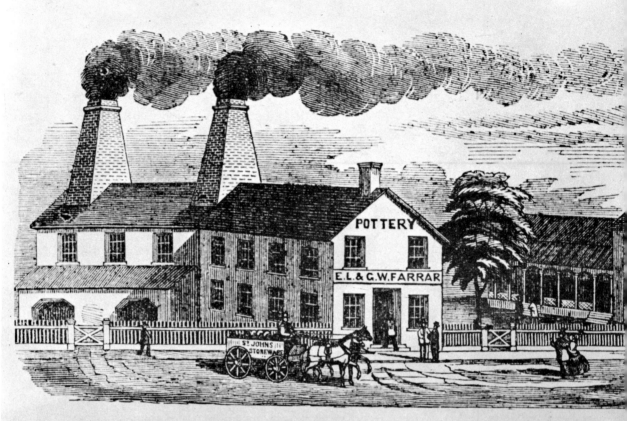

HE WILL KEEP ON HAND

ROOT & GINGER BEER

SNUFF JAR

FIRE CLAY AND SAND, FIRE BRICK, PORT

VERMONT FLINT ENAMELLED

SCOTCH ENAMELLED EART

All orders addressed to him, or to T. C. WATSON, 22 Lemoine Street, Montreal, or TF Quebec, will be thankfully received and promptly supplied.

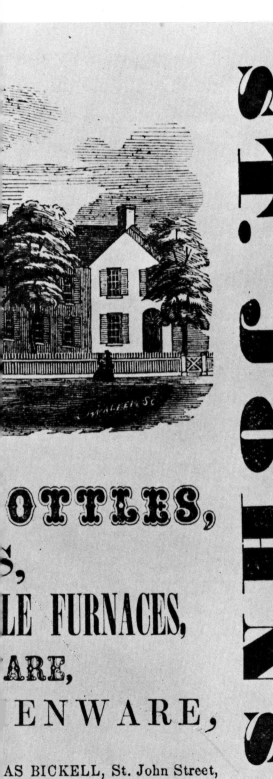

2 gallon jug, with a slip-trailed decoration of a huge sunflower. The flower is similar to designs on O. L. Ballard pottery from Burlington, Vermont, and the jug may be from the Ballard Pottery at St. Johns, Quebec, c. 1858-1860. It is stamped only with a merchant's mark, WELLS & AUDY/MARCHAND EPICIERS/No. 54 56 RUE TS PIERRE/BASSE VILLE/Quebec. Height 14".

4 gallon crock, brush-painted in blue with a motif of a bunch of grapes, and marked CORNWALL/POTTERY, C. W. "Cornwall Pottery" was another name used by Flack and Van Arsdale, c. 1880-85. Height 11".

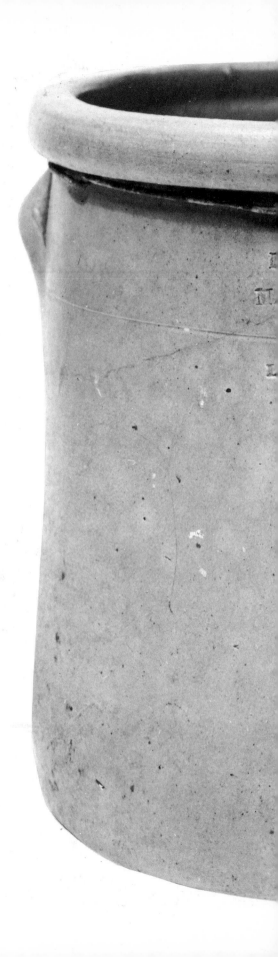

2 gallon crock, probably from Cornwall or the Farrar Pottery
c. 1870-90, with a simple bird decoration and a merchant's mark
FORTIN & MORENCY/MARCHAND EPICIERS/COIN DES
RUES LOUS/LE FORT & ST. PIERRE. Height 9⅝".

Jug and tall jar, made and marked by FLACK & VAN ARSDALE/
CORNWALL, O., c. 1880-1900. Human figures as decorations are
very rare on Canadian stoneware. The bird on a branch with
scrolls, on the jar, is a characteristic motif of the Cornwall Pottery.
Heights, Left 13¾", Right 16½".

5 gallon butter churn, with a brushed-blue decoration of flowers, and a rare marking, MORTON, GOOLD & CO./BRANTFORD, C.W. The partnership of Justin Morton and F. P. Goold at the Brantford Pottery lasted only a few months in 1859; followed by Goold acquiring the business. Height 17½".

1 gallon jug marked F. P. GOOLD/BRANTFORD (1859-1867),
with a design in blue of a duck floating on water. Height 11".

The kiln furniture for salt-glazed stoneware typically consisted of setting-tiles and wedges, the tiles used for separating pots horizontally. On the left are sectional and ring tiles, used as bases for stacks of pottery. Three hand-formed lumps in the left-centre had an unknown use, and to the right-centre are flat and disc tiles, for separating the bases and openings of crocks and jugs; one such tile adheres to the rim of a jug sherd. The wedges on the right were used for stabilizing stacks of pottery.

One of the most elaborate known examples of Canadian salt-glazed stoneware, this water-cooler is fully decorated with incised birds, two horses, and a man on horseback, separated by trees. All incised lines were filled with blue glaze, applied as a powder before firing. The cooler is not marked, but from decorative characteristics was made at the Brantford Pottery during the Goold period, 1859-67. Height 15".

School-house inkwells, roughly made and lined with brown slip, recovered during excavations at the Brantford Pottery. The inkwells, of which numbers were found, date c. 1870-1883. Heights average 1 inch; diameters range from 1¾" to 2¼".

Outdoor jardiniere, in three sections and on a separate base. The urn has three identically moulded and applied Royal Crests on the upper section, and smaller applied eagles on each side of the base. The whole structure was originally salt-glazed, and more recently painted. Made by Henry Schuler at the Brantford Pottery, c. 1885-90. Height 42".

Price list card of stoneware still being made by the Farrar Pottery as late as 1926. The pottery closed shortly after the death of George Farrar, grandson of the founder, in 1927.

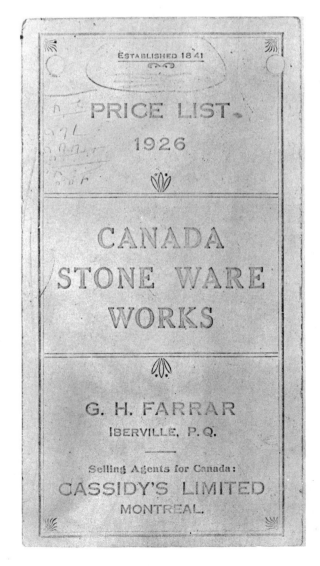

ESTABLISHED 1841

PRICE LIST.

1926

CANADA
STONE WARE
WORKS

G. H. FARRAR

IBERVILLE, P.Q.

Selling Agents for Canada:

CASSIDY'S LIMITED

MONTREAL.

Pots a Beurre avec couvercles	BUTTER POTS COVERED	Per Doz.
	10 Gallons	$54 00
	8 "	4 00
	6 "	2 00
	5 "	24 00
	4 "	20 00
	3 "	16 00
	2 "	12 00
	1½ "	10 00
	1 "	8 00
	½ "	5 00
Pots a Feve	BEAN POTS	
	2 Gallons	12 00
	1½ "	9 00
	1 "	7 00
	¾ "	6 00
	½ "	5 00
	¼ "	4 00
Cruches, mesure Imperial	JUGS, IMPERIAL MEASURE	
	2 Gallons	12 00
	1 "	7 00
	½ "	5 00
Pots a Sirop	SYRUP JARS	
	2 Gallons	12 00
	1 "	8 00
	½ "	6 00
Pots a Fleurs	FLOWER POTS	
	2 Gallons	9 00
	1½ "	7 00
	1 "	5 00
	½ "	4 00
	¼ "	3 00
	⅛ "	2 00
Barrates avec couvercles	CHURNS, WITH COVERS	
	8 Gallons	42 00
	6 "	28 00
	5 "	24 00
	4 "	20 00
	3 "	16 00
	SPITOONS	
No. 1		24 00
" 2		18 00
" 3		10 00
" 4		8 00
" 5		6 00

N.B.—All Goods sold F.O.B. Iberville, 3% 30 days.
CRATES AND STRAW EXTRA.
Selling Agents for Canada:
CASSIDY'S LIMITED. MONTREAL.

Tonic and beer bottles in different versions. The left-hand 12-sided bottle is marked DR. CRONK, the mark, though the bottle is probably English, of an Ontario patent-medicine dealer. The left-centre beer bottle, brown slip covered and probably from the Hart Pottery, is marked W. HALL KINGSTON. The right-centre piece, also a beer bottle, is stamped I. STRATFORD/WHITBY. The right bottle, actually a handled jug, is from the Schuler and McGlade Pottery in Paris, Ontario, and is marked RETURN TO/ J. H. AHRENS/WINE & SPIRIT MERCHANT/PARIS, ONT. All of the bottles date c. 1870-80. Heights, Left to Right 10⅝", 10", 9⅝", 8⅞".

RETURN TO
J. H. AHRENS
WINE & SPIRIT MERCHANT
PARIS ONT

Elaborate tall salt-glazed water filter, designed by T. Plummer of Toronto, and made at the Brantford Pottery, c. 1849-57, and marked MORTON & CO./BRANTFORD, C.W. The piece is covered with moulded and separately applied relief motifs, some identical to the decorations on other unmarked early Brantford slip-cast pitchers, and has the faces from moulded dogs as handles. Height 24¾".

For firing, stoneware vessels were stacked in the kiln base-to-base and rim-to-rim. When stacked in this manner, bases, usually rims, and insides of vessels are not exposed to salt-glazing. Such a stack requires separators and additional support, provided by ring or sectional tiles (a), on which stack is based, flat disc or elongated tiles (b) between the necks of jugs or bottles, and wedges (c) at two or three points on each vessel to separate the vertical stacks.

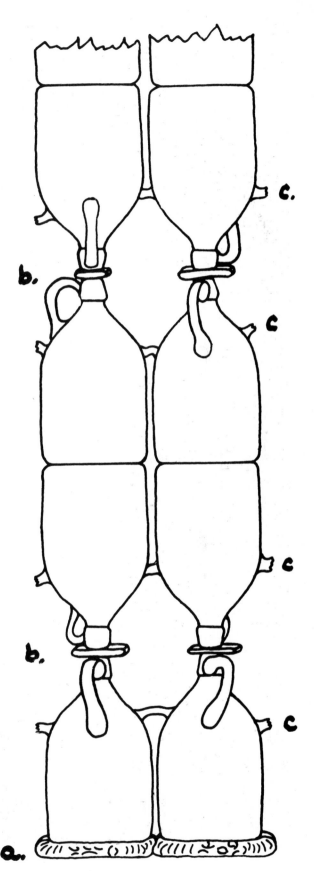

Potato storage jar and batter-jug. The jar is marked "Pottoes"
and a 2 gallon figure in blue glaze, and stamped G. I. LAZIER/
PICTON, C.W. The 3 quart batter-jug is decorated with a blue
bird characteristic of the Hart Pottery during Lazier's period
(1868-87), but is unmarked. The "C.W." mark on Lazier potter
(pre-H.B. & L.) was evidently never changed to Ontario. Heights,
Left 11", Right 8".

Jar and saucepan, the jar brown slip coated and marked E. E. BERUBE & CO./OYSTERS, probably a Montreal merchant. The salt-glazed saucepan, a rare form, is marked W. L. BASTIAN/ IMPORTER/MONTREAL. Both pieces are probably from the Flack & Van Arsdale Pottery at Cornwall, Ontario, or the Farrar Pottery at Iberville, Quebec, c. 1870-90. Heights, Left 6¾", Right 3¼".

Stoneware flowerpots with integral saucers, the left and right pieces with rims dipped in brown slip, but unglazed. Both are from the Brantford Pottery, c. 1870-80. The centre flowerpot is finished with brown slip on the exterior, and may be a later Brantford type. Heights, Left to Right 5", 5¾", 4".

Stoneware canning jars, types commonly used in the late 19th and early 20th century, with various patent sealing systems. The left-hand jar, brown slip coated, is marked "Glass Bros./London, Ont./Pat'd July 1901". The centre piece, originally sealed with a wooden stopper in wax, has a white-slip coated body and yellow-glazed shoulder, and is marked BRANTFORD/CANADA on the base. The right jar, with white body and brown shoulder and top, has its top marked in relief "THE WEIR/pat'd March 1, 1892". Heights, Left to Right 5⅝", 6¾", 6⅜".

8 Manufacturing – Rockingham and Yellow-ware

The individual commercial craft-based potter in Canada was always severely limited in the variety and complexity of what he could produce. Reliance on locally available red-firing clays; the impossibility of competing with mass-produced importations; and the lack of available capital or any established technological base: all were factors which seriously hindered the development of a modern ceramics industry in Canada and for a long time restricted native manufacture to the level of hand-made earthenware. A reasonable case can be made for the idea that a small and scattered population and market delayed the establishment of native industry, and hence Canada's entry into the English and North American industrial revolution. Canada was also, however, a British colony and as such a protected British marketing area. There is also some reason to feel that the British ceramics industry, by its marketing practices, including at-cost or less-than-cost dumping aided by preferential duties, deliberately discouraged the development of a home industry as long as possible.

The transition in the Canadian pottery industry from the craft system, dependent on human skill and labour alone, to the rudiments of a factory system based on invested capital and technology, began apparently at the Brantford Pottery with the introduction in the late 1850's of moulded and slip-cast wares.

The difference was a rather great one. Production of moulded and cast wares depended on equipment and a factory system. With moulds and mechanical processes involved, it was possible to turn out in great quantity much more complex vessels than any single potter could possibly make by hand. By introducing specialized functions, the whole production process was also made much more efficient, with different people carrying out entirely separate operations toward the final assembly of the ultimate object.

Sectional moulding, and assembly from various component parts, was an essential technique for producing one pottery type that became extremely popular in 19th century North America—the figure or patterned wares with integral decorative motifs standing in relief.

This moulded pottery was most commonly produced as teapots, pitchers, and spittoons, and very often was covered with that ubiquitous 19th century glaze known in different areas as "Rockingham," "Bennington," or "spatter."

The term "Rockingham" is perhaps most apt, and most commonly used. The finish on much of this moulded pottery, in its simplest form, appears as a spattering, dripping, or thin wash of brown slip over the buff, yellow, or reddish pottery body, and is in fact just that. To create the effect, brown slip was shaken, dripped, sponged, splashed, or poured onto the body of a formed pot, usually over dried green-ware, but sometimes after biscuit firing. Then a covering glaze was applied, always over biscuit-fired pieces. This was usually a lead oxide, but on finer pieces was a flint enamel (silica). Finally, the pottery was fired a second time.

The North American spatter or Rockingham glaze seems to be a simplification of the tortoise-shell finish on Whieldon pottery of the 18th century. Legend has it that the spattering and glazing technique was developed at the pottery of the Marquis of Rockingham, but in fact it became far more popular in North America during the last half of the 19th century than it ever did in England. The term Bennington, commonly applied to wares of this type, comes from the vast production, and present collector popularity, of the pottery produced in the mid 19th century at Bennington, Vermont. Though it is not particularly justified, the term Bennington in the U.S., and Canada as well, has come to denote all of the brown spatter wares.

The earliest attempts at producing moulded or cast wares in the U.S. occurred in the 1760's, but successful industrial moulding, in combination with brown spatter as a finish, seems to have been introduced only about 1830, in New Jersey. It quickly became popular in the United States, and by 1850 was being produced as common and inexpensive tableware by dozens of pottery factories from New Jersey to Ohio. Although very little American pottery was being imported into Canada at that time, it still was not long until pattern-decorated Rockingham-glazed pottery became popular here and native Canadian production began.

Moulded stoneware spittoons, the left piece covered with brown slip and stamped MORTON & CO. (1850-57, Brantford, Ontario) in the base. The piece on the right is Rockingham-glazed, and stamped in the base FLACK & VAN ARSDALE/CORNWALL, C.W. Height, Left 4¼", Right 4⅜".

The first producer of sectional-moulded ceramics in Canada was probably Justin Morton at the Brantford Pottery, in the late 1850's. Though Morton was primarily a salt-glazed stoneware maker, several moulded spittoons and two large pitchers bearing the mark MORTON & CO. on the base are known. John Brown, of Bowmanville, Ontario, in 1859 patented a pattern for a large moulded dog figure, one of the earliest ceramic patents in Canada. Then in 1860 the Cap Rouge Pottery (Howison, Pye & Chartre) was organized at Cap Rouge, Quebec, under an experienced factory manager, Philip Pointon, specifically to manufacture moulded Rockingham and yellow-ware. Competition increased from that point on, and the height was reached about 1890, with over ten Canadian moulded-ware factories in operation. One of the largest was the Robert Campbell Pottery of Hamilton, Ontario, established about 1880 to produce Rockingham and yellow-wares. After 1900 the company became first R. Campbell & Sons, Ltd., and finally Canadian Potteries, Ltd., but it continued producing household ceramics, including Rockingham and yellow-wares, into the 1930's.

Another large producer was the Brantford Pottery, which manufactured a very wide range of moulded wares after W. E. Welding took control in 1873. Rockingham-glazed and yellow-wares predominated until after 1890, with the striking beaver and maple leaf teapots being perhaps the best known today. After 1890 the factory also began making blue and green-glazed household wares, as well as multi-colored pieces in an *art nouveau* fashion, which continued in production until the company closed in 1907.

Several different moulding techniques were used for various pottery types, depending on the degree of complexity. The most sophisticated was slip-casting, generally used for producing hollow-wares such as teapots, pitchers, and patterned spittoons, as well as the common moulded dog or King Charles Spaniel figures (see chapter 6). For slip-casting, hollow moulds were prepared of plaster of paris, in two half-sections that could be separated.

Clay mixed to a fluid consistency was poured into a closed mould, which was then tipped back and forth evenly, so the slip would contact all inner surfaces. The plaster absorbed water from the slip, stiffening the clay in closest contact with the mould sides, and essentially formed a hard clay shell to the configuration of the mould. Excess liquid slip was poured off. The longer the slip remained in the mould, the thicker became the wall of clay next to the mould surface, until the plaster had absorbed all the water it could hold. After a short period of further drying, the mould could be opened and the cast clay shell removed. Since clay shrinks slightly in drying, mould and casting usually separated easily. The plaster mould, after the absorbed water dried off, was then ready for casting again.

A vessel as complex as a teapot typically required four moulds, each as two sections, to cast all of its components–the body, the spout, a handle, and the lid. These parts were cast separately, and probably by different people. After seams had been smoothed, the various units were then assembled and attached with the same slip that had been used for casting. Once dried, the assembled vessels could finally be glazed and fired exactly as any wheel-turned pot.

One virtue of plaster moulds was and is that they can be easily and cheaply made up from any original form–a clay or wooden master, or even a sharply detailed existing pot if a factory felt inclined to copy. Moulds were also usually made up in duplicate, for to be truly efficient one worker used from twelve to twenty, casting in some while others dried.

The moulded Rockingham industry produced little in the way of truly fine wares, or specially moulded or glazed pieces, but rather concentrated on the manufacture of utilitarian pottery in quantity and at competitive prices. Very little of this pottery, unfortunately for the present-day collector, in Canada was marked in any way until after 1890. Earlier marked pieces usually seem to have been special examples, for the markings were very often incised in script, by hand.

Most Rockingham-glazed pottery encountered today in Canada is probably of Canadian origin. American wares of this type were not imported in any quantity. It is much more difficult, however, as with unmarked earthenware, to

Unmarked roughly moulded pitcher, with a relief motif of a woman playing a lyre, and finished in brown slip. Brantford Pottery, c. 1855-60. Height 8¼".

identify specific pieces with their manufacturers. We know the products of some factories only through archaeological excavations or site examinations, such as at Brantford and Cap Rouge, and of others through existing early catalogues, such as the Campbell Pottery.

The patterns made at different pottery factories, however, are not yet as completely identified as are Canadian glass patterns (nor have they been subject to as much misinformation). As with pressed or moulded glass patterns, it is also possible that more than one pottery factory may have used identical moulds to produce identical pieces, though this appears unlikely.

Some Rockingham patterns, however, were patented, and even where different factories turned out pieces using the same motif—such as Beaver and Maple Leaf or Rebecca at the Well teapots—there were obvious variations. There is no real indication so far that Canadian factories manufactured any but forms unique to each.

A second type of moulded and mass-produced utility ware, very popular in Canada as well as England and the United States, was the so-called yellow or cane-ware. Unlike Rockingham, yellow-ware was limited to open vessels—bowls and baking dishes, with a few rare exceptions. The basic finish was a lead glaze, usually with a very small percentage of iron oxide, over the white or grey-firing body.

Though very often finished plain and undecorated, in its most common form as heavy kitchen bowls yellow-ware was typically banded with lines of white or brown slip. The banding was applied, by slip-cup or brush, on green-ware before biscuit-firing, after which the glaze was added. Decorated with a mossy pattern of diffused blue or black glaze over a wide white band, the pottery was known as mocha.

Mocha, in many forms, was largely imported from England, where it had been made since the 1820's. It was, however, after 1870 also produced in limited quantity in Canada; the Brantford, Ontario, and Cap Rouge, Quebec, potteries, both of which manufactured quantities of banded yellow bowls, are the only two factories known to have done mocha diffusions in the English manner. On Canadian pieces a drop of cobalt blue or manganese black glaze was dropped on a wide band of air-dried but unfired white slip. Then a drop of turpentine was placed on the glaze, causing it to flow and diffuse to form the typical mossy decorative pattern.

Since yellow-wares were generally open bowls, the moulding process was relatively simple. A simplified and relatively automatic production process known as jiggering, suitable for production of bowls and plates, was in use in Canada by 1880 and was employed universally by 1900. For jiggering, a solid mould for the exterior of the piece revolves on a wheel. Clay rolled in sheets is pressed into this mould, taking the exterior shape. Then a sharp edged template is lowered onto the mould, shaving off excess clay to the ultimate vessel wall thickness, and forming the interior shape. The jiggering process thus was essentially the same as cutting clay on a vertical lathe, and it made possible a very rapid production.

There does not seem to be any real reason for the limited shape variety of yellow-ware, except perhaps that Rockingham was acceptable at table, while the yellow was kitchen pottery. Both Rockingham and yellow-ware were moulded of the same high-firing earthenware or stoneware—only the finishes were different. All moulded-ware factories, in fact, produced identical bowls and dishes both Rockingham and yellow-glazed, the finish optional and the price the same.

Rockingham and yellow-glazed slip-cast or moulded household pottery remained in fashion well into the 20th century, until it finally declined in popularity in the 1920's and 30's. Because of its long production range, much of this pottery is hard to date precisely, and some is perhaps not as antique as we might like to think. Still, slip-cast Rockingham is a closed-ended type, no longer produced. Fascinating as evidence of the beginnings of ceramic technology in Canada, it is also extremely varied, and some forms are still relatively common. More work is needed on identification of patterns, but even the myriad known forms offer a special, and reasonably fresh, field for collectors.

The base of the Cap Rouge moulded pitcher, with the marking in incised script, CAP ROUGE POTTERY.

Pitcher with relief motifs of standing cranes or herons and foliage, brown slip covered, and marked "Cap Rouge Pottery", c. 1880-90.

Table pitchers, moulded with very similar but not identical leaf, grape, and fern motifs in relief. The pitchers are Rockingham-glazed but unmarked. They may be products of the Cap Rouge Pottery or of the Farrar Pottery, St. Johns, c. 1870-80, although there is no basis for any direct attribution. Heights, Left to Right 8¾", 7⅞", 7¼".

Rockingham-glazed teapot, of dense buff earthenware with relief moulding of a Rebecca at the Well pattern, from the Cap Rouge Pottery, c. 1860-1900, Cap Rouge, Quebec. On the left is a biscuit-fired sherd from the site, and on the right a glazed sherd. Height 6½".

Sherds and lids of the Brantford beaver and maple leaf patterned teapot, c. 1883, excavated at the Brantford Pottery, 1967.

Teapot with a beaver and maple leaf pattern, and a moulded beaver as the lid finial, Rockingham-glazed stoneware, Brantford Pottery, but unmarked, c. 1883. Height 6″, including lid 7½″.

Variant form of the Brantford Pottery beaver and maple leaf patterned teapot. This example, also unmarked, was probably manufactured c. 1875-80, and is a clumsier and heavier version of the preceeding piece. Height, including lid 7⅝".

Stoneware Rockingham-glazed teapot with a beaver and maple leaf pattern in relief, unmarked but western Ontario (possibly Campbell or Brantford), c. 1880-90. The broken cover finial has been replaced with a riveted metal loop. Height, including lid, 10½".

Rockingham-glazed pitcher, with a pattern of a beaver and maple leaves, and ribbed base section, very similar to the preceding teapot. The piece is unmarked, but is possibly from the Brantford or Campbell Pottery, c. 1885-95. Elizabeth Collard in Nineteenth Century Pottery & Porcelain in Canada *illustrates a similar but not identical piece in yellow glaze. Height 10¾".*

Shell-patterned Brantford spittoons, of slip-cast stoneware, Rockingham-glazed. Brantford Pottery, c. 1880-83. Heights, Top 3", Bottom 4¾".

Red earthenware jardiniere, as a single unit, Rockingham-glazed, from the Dion Pottery, c. 1890-1900. Height 22".

Covered red earthenware tobacco jar, with a separate heavy base unit. Relief figures of musicians and dancers circle the jar, and three moulded sea serpents brace the cover finial. The piece is Rockingham-glazed, and was made at the Dion Pottery, Ancienne Lorette, Quebec, c. 1880-1900. Base diameter 12½".

Rockingham-glazed moulded teapots, both Quebec, c. 1880-1900. The left piece, of a dense white earthenware with two cherubs in relief, is from the Bell Pottery, Quebec. The right-hand red earthenware piece has a motif of a single cherub surrounded by grapes, and may be from the Dion Pottery. Heights, Left 6½", Right 7¼".

Moulded stoneware utility bowl with Rockingham glaze, unmarked, with a pouring spout. Campbell Pottery, Hamilton, Ontario, c. 1880-1900. Diameter, 9¾".

Late Brantford slip-cast spittoon, c. 1894-1906, with a green Rockingham glaze, and marked BRANTFORD/CANADA on the base. Height, 5¼".

Bowl and covered chamber pot, both of slip-cast stoneware with a spattered green glaze, and marked BRANTFORD/CANADA on the bases, the mark of the Brantford Stoneware Mfg. Co., Ltd. Brantford Pottery, c. 1894-1907. Height, Left 11", Diameter, Right 13¾".

Fluted stoneware bowls, Rockingham-glazed, manufactured at the Brantford Pottery and marked on the bases BRANTFORD/ CANADA, c. 1894-1906. Diameters, Left 8¼", Right 9⅜".

20th century Rockingham, a cream pitcher and two bowls, all from and marked by Medalta Potteries Ltd., Medicine Hat, Alberta. Medalta Potteries used a native Alberta stoneware clay, one of the only two known deposits in Canada, discovered about 1910. Height, Left 5¾"; Diameters, Centre 4¾", Right 8⅛".

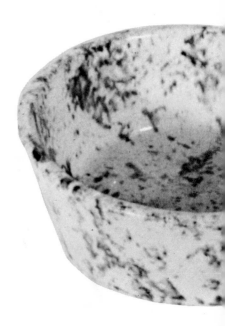

Small utility or soup bowls, c. 1873-83, excavated at the Brantford Pottery. The banding is of white slip over unfired buff stoneware. The bowls were biscuit-fired after banding, and then glazed and re-fired. Other excavated sherds had mixed white and brown banding. Heights, Left 3¼", Centre, 3½", Right 2⅝".

Utility bowls, of buff earthenware. The banding is of white, brown and blue slip, all applied over the body in an unfired state. The bowls were then biscuit-fired, and finally lead-glazed and re-fired. Quebec, Cap Rouge Pottery, late 19th century. Diameters, Left 9⅜", Right 8¼".

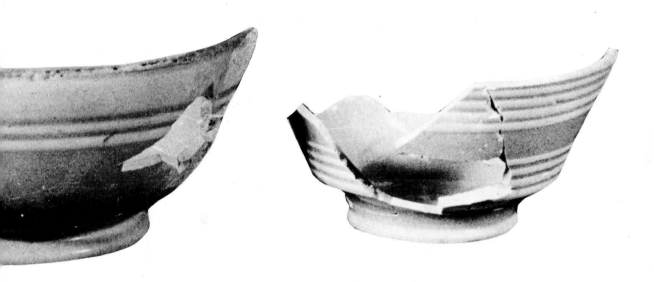

Bed Pans FRENCH SLIPPER—ROCK

Our Bed Pans in the French Slipper shape are old reliable lines, and are made in the Rock (dark Brown) and Cane (Yellow) glaze.

	per doz.
Rock	$17.90
Cane	16.50

Comfort Bed or Douche Pan

This is a Bed or Douche Pan, and is the most comfortable and useful article of its kind made. It has a large capacity, is easily cleaned, and is perfectly sanitary. Price is higher than for the Slipper shape, but it is worth the difference.

Comfort Bed Pan $27.50 per doz.

Urinals—Made in two shapes. Finished in Cane (Yellow) glaze. They are sanitary, easily cleaned, and are used in the most particular homes and hospitals.

Male or Female $11.45 doz.

Our Ware has a Reputation.

Scollops
WHITE LINED

We also make Scollops in Cane (Yellow) finish on outside and white inside. These make the nicest baking dishes one could wish for, and also look well for table service.

Diameter	Price
6 inches	$2.55 per doz.
7 "	3.15 " "
8 "	4.25 " "

Bakers
ROCK OVAL OR OBLONG

One of the most useful dishes is a Baker, and our range of sizes in this article is large enough to fill all requirements. These are finished in our Mottled Rock glaze, and like all of our other Ware are fire-proof, so that they will withstand the great heat to which they are subjected while baking in kitchen ovens. These are made both in Oval and Oblong shape.

Diameter	Price
6 in.	$2.15 per doz.
7 "	2.40 " "
8 "	2.75 " "
9 "	3.15 " "
10 "	3.60 " "
11 "	4.70 " "
12 "	5.20 " "

Rock Pie Plates

The particular cook uses our pie plates for particularly good pies. These plates will stand the heat of the oven, and we can recommend them for use in the best kitchens. Finished in Mottled Rock glaze.

Diameter	Price
7 inches	$1.50 per doz.
8 "	1.90 " "
9 "	2.15 " "
10 "	2.35 " "

Our Ware will bear comparison.

Catalogue of Canada Potteries, Ltd., of about 1920-25. Some pieces mentioned had been in production by the predecessor Campbell Pottery for several decades, and a number of items were still available in either Rockingham (Rock) or yellow (cane) finish.

Champion Teapots

The old reliable has been a favorite on the market for many years, and is finished in our Rock (dark brown) glaze.

The "Champion" Teapot has a lock lid, and has a nicely embossed pattern on the sides. It is made in six sizes, as follows:

Size	Capacity		Price	
42 s	5	cups	$3.30 per doz.
36 s	7	"	3.50 " "
30 s	8½	"	4.25 " "
24 s	11	"	5.25 " "
18 s	13	"	6.65 " "
12 s	16	"	8.25 " "

Our Ware is Fire-Proof.

Globe Teapots

This shape of Teapot is very popular, and is desired by those who like plain, neat ware.

The "Globe" Teapot is well finished, and takes a beautiful smooth glaze. It is made in plain Rock (dark brown) color, and the sizes range from individual to family size.

Size	Capacity		Price	
60 s	2	cups	$2.70 per doz.
48's	3	"	2.90 " "
42 s	4	"	3.20 " "
36 s	5	"	3.50 " "
30 s	7	"	4.25 " "
24 s	9	"	5.20 " "
18 s	13	"	6.65 " "

Our Tea Pots Pour Well.

Banded bowl of hard buff earthenware or soft stoneware, with a crude mocha pattern in blue over a wide white band, and brown and white slip bands. Found in Quebec and probably from the Cap Rouge Pottery, c. 1870-80. Diameter, 9⅝".

212

Yellow-glazed bowls, with narrow brown bands, and each with a
wide white band overlaid with mocha diffusions in blue.
Brantford Pottery, c. 1875-1890. Diameters, Left 15", Right 9".

Moulded Brantford utility bowls, c. 1880. The yellow-glazed piece on the left was excavated at the factory in 1967; the identical right bowl is Rockingham-glazed. Diameters, Left, 5⅓", Right 6½".

9 Whitewares and Porcelain

Canada is even today filled with a great variety of early whiteware, the universal serving and table pottery of the 19th century—a visit to any antique shop or country auction confirms this. Variously called "ironstone china," "stone chinaware," or "white granite," this white, highly vitrified, and extremely durable all-purpose tableware was developed in England in the early 19th century, essentially from processed clays containing a high porportion of silica. Josiah Spode, the great Staffordshire potter, first developed about 1803 a material which he marketed as "stone china," and which within a decade virtually replaced earlier and less durable creamware and pearlware. Then Charles Mason, Spode's nephew by marriage, a decade later developed a slightly different body which he patented in 1813 as "ironstone china".

It was basically this material, copied by numbers of other manufacturers, which was so heavily imported into Canada throughout the 19th century, in every possible form from plates and platters to gravy boats and huge tureens, marked with such names as Mason, Adams, and Podmore, Walker. The "stone china" or "ironstone" varied greatly in quality through the century. At its best it was light and finely formed, a near porcelain, and at its worst heavy and crude, ceramically close to a natural stoneware. This basic English whiteware was also the body which underlay a vast range of transfer-printed designs, some developed exclusively for export markets, including many specially for Canadian sales appeal. These, however, and the other English wares, do not lie within the scope of this book.

Canadian potters, and the Canadian ceramics industry generally, for reasons stated earlier, until very late in the century were in no position to experiment with anything but wholly natural clays or with any highly sophisticated ceramics. There is no evidence that anyone in Canada attempted to produce "stone china" commercially, or any form of porcelain, before the 1870's.

Then in 1873 George Whitefield Farrar, of the Burlington, Vermont, stoneware-making family and owner of the Farrar factory at St. Johns, Quebec, established the St. Johns

White ironstone serving dish, platter, and nut or candy dishes, all made and marked by the St. Johns Stone Chinaware Company, St. Johns, Quebec, 1873-93. Lengths, Left to Right 7¾", 10½", 16¼", 7¼", 7¾".

Stone Chinaware Company, with initial capital from the Macdonald family of St. Johns. The new factory was set up specifically to produce white tablewares in direct competition with the English factories. The story of this company—its fires and economic troubles—is related at length in Elizabeth Collard's *Nineteenth Century Pottery and Porcelain in Canada.* From a technical and production aspect, at least, the company was a success, and for over twenty years produced a great variety of wares, from soap dishes to tablewares and full dinner services to huge and elaborate slop jars.

Most of the "stone china" made at St. Johns was white, slip cast in moulds, and often with sharp and well defined relief patterns. Better pieces were decorated with coloured enamel bands, usually a dark red, a royal blue, or gilt, in various combinations and occasionally greens and silver lustre. All of the St. Johns whitewares, too, seem to have been marked on the base with an underglaze stamp in black enamel.

There appear to be numbers of unmarked types of whitewares on the market or in present collections that are popularly attributed to St. Johns with little real authority. Most common perhaps are quantities of crude white bowls with exterior relief patterns of varied beaver and maple leaf designs. These, in particular, are not of as good quality as the known and marked St. Johns pieces, and I rather suspect are of English origin. Generally I would hesitate to attribute to the St. Johns Stone Chinaware Company any piece of white stone china that is not so marked.

The St. Johns factory by 1878-80 was also marketing blue chinaware, the colour achieved not by glazing but by colouring the clay itself before moulding or firing. From a light powder blue in moulded pitchers, the colour varied to a deep and rich blue in sets of table service, pseudo-Wedgwood with tiny white relief appliques. Examination of numbers of pieces also indicates that the actual body material must have varied in its relative components, for some wares, notably two moulded thin-walled pitchers, are actually a soft-paste porcelain, in being translucent to strong light, while other identical pieces are quite opaque.

St. Johns Stone Chinaware Co. pitchers, with relief designs of maple leaves on a stippled background, c. 1880. The left piece, with a light powder blue body, is stamped on the base; the smaller white but otherwise identical piece is unmarked. Both are of a near porcelain, with bodies translucent to strong light. Heights, Left 8½", Right 7".

St. Johns imitation Wedgwood, ironstone with white appliques on blue. These pieces, representative of a larger set, consist of a teapot, sugar bowl and cream pitcher, table bowl, cup and saucer, and dinner and salad plates. All pieces carry on the base the mark of the St. Johns Stone Chinaware Company, St. Johns, Quebec, 1873-93. Diameters, Left 7½" & 9"; Heights, Left to Right, 7", 6¼", 3¼", 6", 3".

Following the losses from a fire in 1893, though the company continued, its economic fortunes were very much in decline, and the St. Johns Stone Chinaware Company finally closed its doors in 1896, not to be revived. Nor was anyone else soon again to attempt commercial production of white "stone china" until 1934, when Sovereign Potters Ltd., of Hamilton, Ontario, once more began production of sets of white tableware. Sovereign claimed this as the first whiteware manufacturing in Canada which, of course, it was not. The surprising fact, however, is the production lag of forty years after the closing of the St. Johns factory.

There was no manufacture of porcelain of any type in Canada in the 19th or early 20th centuries. Again, the problem was probably economic rather than technological, but there is some slight evidence of experimentation with porcelain in the 1860's and '70's. The St. Johns Stone Chinaware Company did in fact produce some porcelain, if we assume the characteristic of translucency to light as a definition. Whether this was accidental we cannot tell, but it is doubtful; more likely the factory intentionally tried some experimental porcelain, which could not be marketed as such or produced in quantity.

In the National Museum of Canada there are two very handsome hand-made soft-paste biscuit porcelain vases, one signed by P.[hilip] Pointon and dated 1871. Pointon had been plant manager of the Cap Rouge Pottery, and from the existence of these pieces evidently was personally experimenting with porcelain, perhaps there, though none is known to have been produced commercially at Cap Rouge.

During excavations at the Brantford Pottery in 1967 we recovered, in a context with the fire of 1883, a very few sherds of biscuit porcelain. Since ceramics not actually produced there are found often in pottery sites, this alone means nothing. The Brantford porcelain sherds were biscuit, however, rather than finished and glazed, which raises questions of possible experimentation that we cannot begin to answer at present.

It is perhaps safe to say that, generally speaking, ceramics manufacture during the 19th century in Canada was never able to get wholly beyond dependence on naturally-occurring clays and into the technologically more stable realm of processed clays of absolutely known components. The St. Johns Stone Chinaware Co. was an experiment, a relative technological success but periodically and ultimately a financial failure. It was both too late in its establishment, in that the competition was already dominant, and somewhat ahead of its time for Canada in not quite being able to achieve the technological precision of better capitalized operations elsewhere. And thus Canada had to wait until the 1930's to enter the international ceramics industry fully.

Spittoon, of slip-cast stoneware and glazed a pale blue, c. 1910-30, marked on the base MEDALTA POTTERIES, LTD./MEDICINE HAT/ALBERTA. Height 5¼".

Biscuit-porcelain flower vases, attributed to Philip Pointon at Cap Rouge, Quebec, and perhaps the earliest existing pieces of experimental Canadian porcelain. Both pieces are covered with very well fashioned and applied flowers, rosebuds, and fruit. The tall vase is inscribed in incised script "From P. Pointon to his wife Alzina C. Pointon/Nov. 19, 1871".

10 The Archaeology of Potteries

In the introduction to this book I outlined one of the prime problems in dealing with Canadian ceramics – in a field virtually without previous study, just how do we go about determining what of the great quantity of early pottery in the country is Canadian, and then how do we go on to decide which potteries or factories made which pieces? This is a somewhat more complex problem than it might appear, and the key to it is not so much simply gathering information, but correlating information of different types and from different sources into an understandable form and a coherent package.

In this concept, the study of Canadian pottery, and Canadian antiquities generally, has gotten off on the wrong track, in that a great deal of assumption and guesswork has masqueraded as information (and still does), and much research has been geared to supporting assumptions rather than simply finding out. As cases in point, for many years the common cork-stamped white earthenware popularly called "Port Neuf" was assumed to be Canadian, from the village of Port Neuf, Quebec. It was long ago established that all of this was late 19th century English, Scottish, French, and Dutch importation, and that there never was a pottery at Port Neuf, but it has taken the old supposition a long time to die.

For many years all of the Quebec red-earthen, brown slip spattered wares have been called "Cap Rouge". There is not the slightest question that the Cap Rouge factory produced only yellow-wares and slip-cast Rockingham, and that the pottery generally called "Cap Rouge" is in fact from the Dion Pottery at Ancienne Lorette. Most dealers and collectors still stick to the old attribution and name, and some will resist vociferously any thought to the contrary. I am continually amazed, not so much just at reluctance to change ideas, as at the extremes to which old myths, proved as such, will be defended.

Any research on antiquities, including pottery, requires, first, the documentary approach, the often tedious route of seeking out and compiling all possible written records. This in most cases will provide background on the people and establishments that produced material objects, but only rarely on the objects themselves. The second approach, then, must be the object-oriented one – examining as many existing objects as possible, and determining materials and structure, as much of technology as may be evident, geographical origin and time periods, design forms, cultural derivations, and original uses or applications.

Now comes the real problem. No matter how many pieces of pottery one looks at, the great majority will be removed from the original context and essentially without provenance. A goodly number may be accompanied by a story that is either hopeful assumption or just not so, misleading in any event. It is simply not possible, except with marked pieces and in other rare instances, to determine even nationality, much less specific attribution, solely from studying existing out-of-context pottery and in an absence of earlier work.

One can spend thousands of hours in perfectly productive documentary research on a particular establishment, and learn everything that can be learned about a potter or sequence of potters. None of this, however, usually connects directly with what an actual pottery produced without the lucky, and rare, discovery of an illustrated catalogue or order sheet. Even then, assuming the illustrations are accurate (i.e., photographs, not line engravings), the document is evidence of pottery produced only at the time of its own date.

This same difficulty of achieving documentary-object connection applies whether one is researching pottery, glass, furniture, cast ironwork, or any other sort of object with enough isolated characteristics to make identification at least possible. The craftsmen or workers who produced these objects rarely kept any records other than account books, which were often discarded as soon as they ceased to be needed. Descriptive object records or contemporary written technical records are virtually non-existent. No more today would a sheet-metal worker, for example, ever write down the technique of making a heating duct. He was taught; he knows how; and that is enough.

And so, in studying early pottery, and particularly Canadian pottery from scratch, we arrive sooner or later at the archaeological approach. Digging in the ground is messy work, but the

The Prince Edward Island Pottery (1880-95), excavated in August, 1970. The site is on land of the Agricultural Experiment Station in Charlottetown; the original pottery buildings were torn down about 1903 to convert the land to agricultural use.

only way to arrive fully and accurately at a connection between potters and their products is to seek out the pottery in its original context. This for the most part lies in long buried waster dumps at long forgotten pottery sites.

The actual methodology of digging early potteries is gained only by experience, but for those interested in the details of general historic site archaeological technique, I could only suggest reading something like Ivor Noel Hume's *Historical Archaeology*. In fact I would not recommend that any collector or amateur ever attempt digging a site. This sort of research requires both the background and the resources (money, time, and access to assorted specialized talent) to properly gain all of the information inherent in the site, and to fully interpret and publish the results.

The act of archaeological digging is essentially destructive; i.e., information is not only uncovered but physically removed. Unless the results are correlated and published the site is simply destroyed and useless to anyone else. Potting a site haphazardly to recover a few artifacts or a batch of sherds for one's personal collection or ego gratification is, to me, a criminal act.

The first prerequisite of digging is the documentary research – putting together as complete as possible a picture of a pottery establishment and its potters from all available sources. Tax records, land transfer records, birth and death records, early newspaper accounts, city, county, and provincial directories and atlases, as well as all manner of other diverse sources, must be explored thoroughly and exhaustively. Ideally, this historical background should be completed before one ever puts a shovel in the ground.

Once a site has been chosen for digging it must be located, usually first by survey descriptions and map placement. Then comes the problem of actually locating the site on the ground, which can be either extremely difficult or on occasions absurdly easy. In rural areas potteries were often abandoned and the buildings were either demolished or allowed to fall to ruin. As grass and weeds annually grew and died, and as autumn leaves fell, the foundations of structures and heaps of waster pottery gradually became covered with decomposed organic

Large fragment of a mid-18th century Quebec green-glazed earthenware utility bowl, in situ in hard ground at the LeBer site, Ile des Soeurs, Montreal.

material, which in turn became topsoil supporting yet more plant growth. In the absence of human disturbance organic ground build-up of this sort occurs slowly but unceasingly, and within half a century it can easily cover an abandoned site completely.

Assuming the site has lain undisturbed, there will still be visible evidence of former buildings, as mounds outlining foundations, or depressions where there once were holes or pits. Combined frost and root action will also push solid objects to the surface, so that the pottery site typically has quantities of potsherds and brick lying on the surface. A good sampling of ground pick-ups provides a reliable indication of 50 to 75 per cent of the pottery types that could be recovered from digging.

The undisturbed site, while ideal, is also the exception. The hand of man is too possessive for most vacant terrain to remain long untouched. Urban pottery sites, because of more recent excavation and overbuilding, in many cases have been totally destroyed long ago. Either grading or deep overfilling is likewise completely destructive from an archaeological standpoint. Agricultural plowing, stream damming, ditching, orchard planting, light overfilling, heavy machinery traffic which compacts the earth, are all damaging to various degrees. The kiln-site digger, and the historic-period archaeologist generally, simply has to be prepared to deal with disturbed archaeological sites. With the pace of contemporary construction as it is, in setting up digging programs and priorities the researcher often also has to deal first with those sites most threatened with destruction, rather than those that might be the most valuable but are reasonably safe.

Once plans are made to examine a historic archaeological site of any sort, the project leader must be prepared to go all the way—to dig as extensively as is necessary to obtain the full potential from what lies in the ground. This means cleaning, conserving, and reconstructing the artifact recoveries, interpreting the technical evidence (which may mean consulting other specialists), and, finally, writing up and publishing the results. Even the complete and well-done excavation which goes unreported is useless to anyone but the digger.

A 15-inch thick strata of waster pottery at the site of the Burns Pottery, Markham, Ontario.

The author's wife removing a Quebec pot-sherd from compacted ground at the Jacques Le Ber house site, Ile des Soeurs, Montreal (1969). This sherd and others were later reconstructed into a Quebec utility bowl of c. 1750.

Discarded and broken pottery, a section of the deep waster dump at the site of the William Eby Pottery, Conestogo, Ontario.

Crew cleaning the surface of the stone rectangular cross-draft kiln base, at the Gilbert-Marlatt Pottery (c. 1871-95), Port Ryerse, Ontario.

The underground remains of most North American pottery sites consist of three units – production buildings, kilns, and waster dumps. The buildings, generally speaking, are perhaps archaeologically the least important. Any structure could serve as a pottery shop, and pottery shop and storage buildings typically were abandoned and completely empty before they finally fell down or were demolished. As long as we must focus on digging a previous generation's trash and leavings, the empty buildings do not in most cases contain the information we are seeking. With so many 19th century structures still existing, the excavated foundations are usually of little real importance.

The pottery-firing kilns, or as they remain, usually only the kiln floors or bases, are more critical. A buried stone or occasionally a brick kiln base itself indicates, first, the original shape, configuration, and draft type of the kiln, and surrounding rubble often provides clues to the long-destroyed upper structure. There are also usually evident remains or outlines of the fireplace bases, generally two or four in Canadian earthenware kilns, and perhaps indications of inner structure as well.

With the remains of kilns we have often found directly associated evidence of firing techniques and procedures – kiln furniture – the setting tiles, stilts, saggars, and wedges that were once used as containers and as stacking separators for kiln-loads of pottery. Occasionally, too, there will be concentrations of broken sherds of pottery, the vestiges of the last firing, and therefore pottery which, after reconstruction, can be precisely dated to the terminus of the pottery's period of operation.

Waster dumps offer perhaps as much technical information as the kilns themselves, as well as a full range of the actual pottery that an operation produced over the years. These dumps are simply the piles of pottery, rejected for one reason or another, that came to grief somewhere in the production-firing process and were thrown away, usually somewhere adjacent to the kiln. Waster pottery often represented a fair proportion of production, all products of the potters' hands, and was shovelled from the kiln into piles in disappointment at least and likely in anger.

239

The stone base of the domed updraft kiln of the William Eby Pottery. The grid of string, in half-metre squares, is simply an aid to drawing the stonework on graph paper.

Over a span of years these waster piles grew deeper and deeper and spread out sometimes to fill a whole pottery yard; the typical earthenware pottery was hardly a neat or well-kept operation.

Kilns, for archaeological digging, are relatively neat and precise, in that we know pottery or kiln furniture within or immediately beside the kiln must be directly associated with it, and therefore datable to the final firing, or at the outside, to the last few months of operation. Waster dumps, though they are far more productive of sheer masses of material, from the concept of gaining information are also much more difficult to dig, and particularly to interpret, than are kilns.

Covered by sod and mixed with earth that filtered down through the pottery rubble, waster dumps underground, explored by squares or trenches, can appear as a layer three to five feet thick of solid, compacted, broken pottery. This layer must be dug through from the top down, always keeping the entire excavation surface level, for two reasons. First, the dumps always contain many essentially identical pots, all fragmentary, yet after digging we must attempt reconstruction of specific pieces. The various sherds that will later glue together into at least enough of a single piece to provide a complete cross section will tend to lie at about the same level in the dump, as they were shovelled from the kiln. So too, we are always hoping for dating information, and the standard archaeological rule – simply common logic – is that the topmost layers are the last discarded and therefore the latest in date. Pottery waster dumps, however, occasionally present exceptions to this. Thus careless digging in the waster dump or, worse yet, digging vertically (i.e., straight down), would be self-defeating – providing no datable pieces and most likely no reconstructable pottery.

The waster dump must also be dug very carefully and methodically, simply because of the vast amount, and the sameness, of the material. The process is somewhat akin to working on 10,000 jig-saw puzzles, with pieces of each missing, but with 100,000 extra pieces thrown in which do not fit any of the puzzles. No two excavators of potteries agree on the best method

for excavating waster dumps; and anthropologists and historians view each other suspiciously; I am not sure there is any single best method. Some archaeologists will take a complete sampling – every sherd from the full depth of a five-foot square, and depend on acres of table space and hundreds of post-dig hours to make something of it all. I prefer, not having the space or people hours for this, virtually to reconstruct pottery in the ground, trowel in the right hand and a roll of masking tape on the left wrist, with a pile of small paper bags beside me.

While pottery waster dumps produce pottery by the ton and, if sensibly dug whatever the actual method, also good reconstructable pieces, they have one prime drawback in not being associated directly with the kiln. The dump represents, first, only the pottery's rejects, not its production. If we choose to count sherds, and find broken crocks in a proportion of ten to one over broken jugs, we cannot assume the pottery actually made ten times as many crocks as jugs, but only that this is the ratio in the dump

From such a ratio, we could not even decide that ten times as many crocks as jugs were rejected, for waster dumps were not necessarily continuous. From historical references we know that waster pottery was sometimes shovelled directly from the kiln into wagons and hauled off some distance for dumping, thus breaking the continuity of the dump. If over the years the waster dump got too extensive or too deep, it might be moved to a more concentrated pile, or later loaded up and hauled away, perhaps to be dumped in a river. If a dump were abandoned for a few years and then used again, a slight intervening sod layer would appear in the digging as a definite level. If, on the other hand, a dump adjacent to a kiln was not started until ten years after the pottery was established, and then every other kiln-accident load of waster was carted away, and finally the dump was abandoned ten years before the closing of the pottery, we might well never know it from digging. The dump would appear to have been in constant use, as in fact it was during its own period, even though it did not represent the full period of the pottery, and received less than half of the waster actually thrown out during the pottery's operating span. This is an extreme

Firing rubble from the William Eby Pottery, showing how badly pottery could be distorted by the intense heat of over-firing. These large masses are a mixture of twisted and distorted crocks and fire brick, indicating that heat during this firing was high enough to distort and perhaps collapse the kiln itself.

possibility, to be sure, but I use it to illustrate why dating or production interpretations based on waster dumps are touchy at best.

Every piece of pottery thrown on a waster dump usually shows some visible reason for its rejection. Much waster was discarded after its biscuit firing, unglazed and showing all of the body discolouration of over-firing or of reduction firing. Occasionally biscuit-fired pottery was lead-oxide glazed but never re-fired; the glaze then appears as a coating of red-orange powder. Gross over-firing resulted in bent, buckled, and distorted pots. The collapse in firing of part or all of a kiln-load of stacked pottery leaves evidence of multiple pieces, or sherds of pieces, fused together, usually by glazes, but occasionally even as biscuit. All of the kiln-furniture, the stilts, saggars, pins, and such, turn up in quantity in the waster heaps. Inappropriate glaze mixtures, or glazes fired at too hot a temperature, appear bubbled or discoloured. Structurally weak designs show consistent fractures in the same places, and even finished and marketed versions likely broke in the same way when housewives eventually dropped them.

When combined and correlated with later chemical analyses of glazes and pottery bodies, this information gleaned from waster dumps and kilns provides a very good overall picture of the technical level of the pottery operation. We can determine ideal, and extreme, firing temperatures by modern controlled re-firing, as well as, by analysis, the exact percentages of glaze components. In the end it is not difficult to see why the average earthenware producer could not possibly compete, for the same products, with the English whiteware factories.

The most positive recovery from early pottery sites, of course, is the pottery itself, and that is what this book is really about. From the sherds, and hopefully from the reconstructions, recovered from a pottery dig, we can be quite sure that this is the pottery actually made there. The recoveries may not indicate all of what was made – forms seldom produced may not show up at all as waster – but there is no reason to doubt that we have most of it. From this, then, we can go on to examine existing pieces (but now based on some context) in the original marketing area of the pottery with some assurance that correlations will appear.

The stage of tying intact early pottery together with the historical background and results of the pottery excavation is the third and final part of the investigation. This does not need to wait until dig analysis is complete; it can well commence as soon as connections appear and, in fact, is likely to begin, intentionally or not, as the dig is in progress.

Any archaeological project attracts visitors, who ask streams of questions and take up inordinate amounts of time, but on pottery excavations they often come bearing pots as well. At the Brantford Pottery, which we had only two weeks to dig, visitors showed up in droves with marked salt-glazed pieces, which added nothing to what we knew, but also with unmarked Rockingham and yellow-glazed pieces which obviously conformed to patterned sherds even before the latter were washed. The William Eby Pottery dig at Conestogo, Ontario, brought in a few by then known Brantford pieces and great numbers of suspected Eby products.

Most visitors are looking for an identification, but few want to give up their treasures, so I have a habit of measuring and photographing on the spot any piece brought to a dig site. During the excavation of the Prince Edward Island Pottery, a great deal of time was spent driving around, photographing marked and suspected P.E.I. Pottery pieces in nearby collections and, with a long lens, even standing earthenware chimney-pots.

The particular value of photographing, and correlating intact pottery to the dig recoveries, is not so much simply to duplicate one complete piece with one complete reconstruction, but rather to use the intact pot to identify the form and shape of unreconstructable sherds – or vice versa. In many cases as well, though a complete reconstruction from sherds is not possible, there is enough to establish in pen and ink drawings what a pot originally was like, without having much of the pot itself. This and an intact piece turning up later will complement each other.

The archaeology of potteries, and perhaps glassworks, is almost a specialty in itself. As well as the experience and precision – essentially the method – necessary for any historic site archaeology, the digging of an object-production site really requires also a prior specific knowledge of the type of object produced. Just a knowledge of excavation procedure is not enough; knowing what to look for, and how to interpret the results, is the important factor. Archaeology cannot be treated as a beginning and end; it is simply an information-gathering method, one of many that must be employed in the total research process. The goal of the exercise still remains a specific contribution to the identification and understanding of Canadian pottery, and of the history and technology of ceramics generally.

Glossary of Terms

Applied decoration – Decorations or motifs of separately moulded or hand-formed pieces of clay, applied to an already formed piece of pottery.

Ball slip – Clay slip made essentially of fine white pipe-clay, generally imported from England.

Biscuit firing; biscuit pottery – Pottery that has been once-fired to harden or fuse the clay body, but which has not been glazed or finished (this requires a second firing at a lower temperature).

Coggle; coggle wheel – A small wheel mounted in a handle, much like a pie-crimper, with a decorative motif intaglio or in relief, for moulding or pressing into a revolving and still plastic pot.

Footed-base – A base as a foot or rim extending below the bottom of a bowl, pitcher, or teapot.

Glaze – A hard glass-like surface or coating for pottery, fused after firing, but typically applied as a liquid. Glazes consist basically of silica, a metallic oxide, and a flux.

Glost or glaze firing – The final firing of pottery to fuse the covering glaze, typically at a lower temperature than the first or biscuit firing.

Green-ware – Pottery formed and air-dried, but not yet fired (and thus still raw clay).

Incised decoration – Decorative motif created by cutting with a fine knife or pointed stylus into a freshly formed but semi-dried pottery vessel. Incised motifs in salt-glazed stoneware were typically glazed in cobalt blue, as a powder wiped into the incised lines.

Lead-glaze – Lead oxide, the metallic base of all early earthenware glazes in Canada, formed a clear or transparent surface when pure, or various translucent colours when mixed with other metallics. Only tin oxide provided an opaque glaze.

Mocha – Yellow-wares decorated with diffusions of glaze drops, usually over a slip band. The diffusion is created by a drop of turpentine or horse urine on a little blue or manganese-black glaze, causing it to flow into a mossy pattern. The name stems from similarity to the pattern of cut moss agates, found on the coasts of the Mocha district of Arabia.

Overlaid rim – A vessel with a rim formed by fully folding over and shaping the top edge of clay as the pot revolves on the potters wheel.

Potters wheel – A round flat working surface,

rotated on a vertical shaft and foot-operated or separately powered, for hand forming round pottery vessels.

Pug-mill – Large tub or barrel, with a central bladed shaft turned by horse power, for breaking up lumps of clay and mixing with water.

Ribs – Wooden scrapers or smoothers, often cut with an outline form, for shaping rims or curves on identical multiple vessels.

Rockingham or spatter glaze – The term for extremely popular 19th century household pottery, with brown slip spattered or flowed over a white or buff pottery body, and overglazed in a separate operation.

Saggar – A container, often of rough fire-clay, for holding pottery too delicate to stack loosely during the firing process. The term is also used for the ring-shaped bases used to support stacks of salt-glazed stoneware in firing.

Salt-glazing – Process of glazing stoneware with a sodium silicate, a chemical combination formed from common salt vaporized in the maximum heat of firing.

Scraffito decoration – Decoration scratched or incised to the body of the pottery, through a covering glaze or slip of a contrasting colour.

Slip – Highly-refined clay, watered to a fluid consistency and used for decorating, surface coatings, and slip-casting.

Slip-casting – The process of casting shells or components of complex vessels, by pouring liquid slip into sectional plaster-of-paris moulds.

Slip-decorating – Decoration with slip of a colour contrasting to the pottery body. Slip could be spattered on (as the Rockingham glaze), painted with a brush for a motif, or, if slightly thicker in consistency, flowed or trailed on the pottery through a quill or straw.

Stilts – Production or kiln furniture for separating pottery in firing with the least marring of glazes. Stilts are generally three branched, with a small point for contact with the pottery on the tip of each branch.

Stoneware – The lowest of vitrified pottery types, from a clay with a high silica content. Stoneware must be fired at a temperature in excess of 2000°F., and most clay used in early North American stoneware came from Amboy, New Jersey.

Thrower – The man who actually hand-formed pottery. The term comes from the necessity of throwing a lump of clay on the potters wheel to be sure it would stick.

Vitrified; vitrification – High-temperature-fired pottery, the clay of which has heat-fused together to form a durable and non-porous body.

Wedges – Hand-formed clay lumps for separating stacks of salt-glazed stoneware during firing.

Bibliography

Barbeau, Marius. "Canadian Pottery," *Antiques*, June 1941, pp. 296-99.

Barber, Edwin Atlee. *Pottery and Porcelain in the United States.* New York, Putnam, 1893.

— — —. *The Tulip Ware of the Pennsylvania German Potters.* Philadelphia, Pennsylvania Museum, 1903.

— — —. *Marks of American Potters.* Philadelphia, Patterson & White, 1904.

— — —. *Salt Glazed Stoneware.* Philadelphia, Pennsylvania Museum, 1906.

Barret, Richard Carter. *Bennington Pottery and Porcelain: A Guide to Identification.* New York, Bonanza, 1958.

Beliard, Bernard. "La poterie au Quebec . . . a partir des pots casses," *Culture Vivante.* August 1969, pp. 19-29.

Blair, C. Dean. *The Potters and Potteries of Summit Country Ohio, 1825-1915.* Akron, Summit Country Historical Society, 1965.

Cardew, Michael. *Pioneer Pottery.* London, Longmans, Green, 1969.

Chandler, Maurice. *Ceramics in the Modern World.* Garden City, N.Y., Doubleday, 1968.

Clement, Arthur W. *Notes on American Ceramics, 1607-1943.* Brooklyn Museum & Brooklyn Institute of Arts and Sciences, 1944.

Collard, Elizabeth A. *Nineteenth-Century Pottery and Porcelain in Canada.* Montreal, McGill, 1967.

Cooper, Ronald G. *English Slipware Dishes, 1650-1850.* London, Alec Tiranti, 1968.

Haggar, Reginald G. *English Country Pottery.* London, 1962.

Hayden, Arthur. *Chats on English Earthenware.* London, Unwin, 1909.

Hobson, R. L. *Catalog of English Pottery* (in the British Museum). London, British Museum, 1903.

Hodges, Henry. *Artifacts: An Introduction to Early Materials and Technology.* London, John Baker, 1964.

Honey, W. B. *The Art of the Potter.* London, Faber & Faber, 1946.

Hough, Walter. "An Early West Virginia Pottery," *Annual Report of the U.S. National Museum (for 1899)*. Washington, D.C., 1901.

Ketchum, William C., Jr. *Early Potters and Potteries of New York State*. New York, Funk & Wagnalls, 1970.

Lambart, Helen H. *19th Century Potteries in the Province of Quebec*. Unpublished ms. report, National Historic Sites Service, Ottawa, 1964.

– – –. *Two Centuries of Ceramics in the Richelieu Valley*. Publication in History No. 1, National Museum of Canada, 1970.

– – –. *The Rivers of the Potters*. Publication in History No. 2, National Museum of Canada, 1970.

Newark Museum Association. *The Work of the Potteries of New Jersey from 1685 to 1876*. Newark, N.J., 1914.

Noel Hume, Ivor. *Historical Archaeology*. New York, Knopf, 1969.

Pageau, Pierrette. *La Poterie au Canada Francais avant 1850*. Unpublished ms., Academie de Quebec, 1967.

Parmelee, Cullen W. *Ceramic Glazes*. Chicago, Industrial Publications, Inc., 1951.

Rackham, Bernard, and Read, Herbert. *English Pottery*. London, Benn, 1924.

Ramsay, John. *American Potters and Pottery*. Boston, Hale, Cushman & Flint, 1939.

Rice, A. H. and Stroudt, J. B. *The Shenandoah Pottery*, Strasburg, Va., Shenandoah Publishing Co., 1929.

Ries, Heinrich. *History of the Clay-Working Industry in the United States*. New York, Wiley, 1909.

Schwartz, Marvin D. *Collectors Guide to Antique American Ceramics*. Garden City, N.Y., Doubleday, 1969.

Scoon, Carolyn. "New York State Stoneware in the New York Historical Society, "New York Historical Society *Quarterly Bulletin*, April 1945, pp. 83-91.

Shackleton, Philip. *Potteries of 19th Century Ontario*. Unpublished ms. report, National Historic Sites Service, Ottawa, 1964.

Spargo, John. *The Potters and Potteries of Bennington*. Boston, Houghton Mifflin, 1926.

Sutermeister, Helen. *Three Early Pottery Sites in Southern Ontario*. Unpublished excavation reports, Royal Ontario Museum, 1969.

Taylor, David and Patrica. *The Hart Pottery, Canada West*. Picton, Ont., Picton Gazette Publishing Co., 1966.

Tracy, Ruth. *The Kulp Pottery Works Site*. Unpublished excavation report, Ontario Archaeological and Historic Sites Board, Toronto, 1967.

Watkins, Lura Woodside. *Early New England Potters and Their Wares*. Boston, Harvard Univ. Press, 1950.

– – –. *Early New England Pottery*. Old Sturbridge Village, 1959.

Webster, Donald Blake. *The Brantford Pottery, 1849-1907*. Royal Ontario Museum, Occasional Paper 13, Toronto, 1968.

– – –. "Pennsylvania and Ontario Earthenwares: A Comparative View." Royal Ontario Museum *Rotunda*, Winter, 1969, pp. 26-33.

– – –.*Early Slip-Decorated Pottery in Canada*. Toronto, Musson, 1969.

– – –. *The William Eby Pottery, Conestogo, Ontario*. Royal Ontario Museum, Occasional Paper 25, Toronto, 1971.

– – –. *Decorated Stoneware Pottery of North America*. Tokyo, Tuttle, 1971.

Williamson, Scott Graham. *The American Craftsman*. New York, Crown, 1940.

Index

Acknowledgements

The last part of a book to be done often seems to be the section in which the writer traditionally credits and thanks all those people who have aided, abetted, supported, and contributed – this is both the writer's pleasure, and self-realization that the job is finished and the manuscript together (in spite of lingering thoughts and doubts). At the same time he accepts all responsibility for errors, omissions, or anything else that may emerge as being wrong with the book – as most certainly he must, for the author alone makes the decisions.

Many of the illustrations in this book are from specialized collections, and my great thanks are due to those people, all of whom are specifically noted in the photograph credits, who permitted me to photograph their prize pieces. Phil Shackleton of Manotick, Ontario, Michel Gaumond of the Ministere des Affaires Culturelles in Quebec, and Harold Pfeiffer of the National Museum of Canada have been particularly helpful and free with their own knowledge. Jeff Miller, Curator of Ceramics at the Smithsonian Institution, both critically read the manuscript for me and on virtually no notice contributed the Foreword.

Being by nature extremely lazy and easily distracted, I find it necessary to write in seclusion and by schedule rather than by mood or whim. My greatest appreciation goes to my wife Lonnie, who has served long hot days both in the trenches on our various excavations, and who took dictated notes as I photographed pottery. For five weeks on a rocky island in Georgian Bay she kept two children and our Newfoundland dog off my back while I concentrated on writing the text and, being more literary than I, she has also gone over and blue-pencilled the manuscript.

Dr. and Mrs. William McGill of Brantford, Ontario, can only be considered accessories before and after the fact. They led us to the Brantford Pottery in 1966, the first I ever dug in Canada, and most recently to the Prince Edward Island Pottery, and have been on several of the excavations. The McGills have also been of constant encouragement, and free with photography of their own extensive collection. Mr. and Mrs. Andrew Brink of Greensville, Ontario, are intensely interested in Ontario earthenware, and led us to the Eby Pottery, excavated in 1967-68. Jean Pierre Cloutier of the National Historic Sites Service, who knows the pottery of the French period better than most people, is also an accessory, and has been continually helpful and encouraging over the years. Lee Warren, Royal Ontario Museum Photographer, did the transparencies for the internal colour plates.

Janet Holmes, Research Assistant in my department at the Royal Ontario Museum, has been on every excavation from Brantford to Charlottetown, has done all of the historical research for archaeological reports, and has corrected galley proofs, all with equanimity. My secretary, Karen Haslan, typed all of this from dictation or island-written rough, some of it through several revisions.

Sources of pieces illustrated, by illustration pages.

Black Creek Pioneer Village, Toronto — 118, 149, 212-13.

Brant County Historical Society, Brantford — 72, 74.

Brink, Mr. & Mrs. Andrew, Greensville, Ont. — 70, 119.

Brook, Mrs. Fern, Simcoe, Ont. — 75.

deVolpi, Mr. Charles, St. Saveur des Monts, P.Q. — 192.

Dunning, Mr. Philip — 117.

Hennessey, Katherine, Charlottetown, P.E.I. — 100, 102-3.

Service d'Archaeologie, Ministere des Affaires Culturelles, Quebec — 40, 42-3, 45-6, 135.

Jordan Museum of the Twenty, Jordan, Ont. — 61.

McGill, Dr. & Mrs. William, Brantford, Ont. — 67, 71, 80-1, 109, 148.

Mellish, Mr. & Mrs. Harry, Charlottetown, P.E.I. — 99.

National Museum of Canada, Ottawa — 53-4, 90, 95, 128, 138, 180, 182-83, 196-98, 221, 225.

North Carolina Dept. of Conservation & Development — 23-4, 26, 30, 35.

Nova Scotia Museum, Halifax — 103.

Royal Ontario Museum, Canadiana Dept. — 33, 47, 50, 53, 55, 59, 61, 67, 75-6, 78-9, 82, 84-5, 88-9, 92-3, 96, 98, 104, 114-15, 117, 142, 144, 150, 152-53, 156-57, 160, 162, 176, 179, 186, 188, 190-91, 195, 200-09, 211, 214-15, 219, 222-24, 229, 231, 233, 235-36, 238, 240, 243.

Shackleton, Mr. Philip, Manotick, Ont. — 64, 68, 77, 84, 108, 122-24, 127, 130-31, 139, 146-47, 164, 166, 168, 170, 175, 184-85, 194.

Sheeler, Mr. John, Toronto — 193.

Smithsonian Institution, Washington, D.C. — 26, 29.

Sorensen, Mrs. Margaret, Port Colborne, Ont. — 63

Webster, D. B., Toronto — 143.

Wilkinson, Mr. & Mrs. Arnold, Toronto — 112, 113.

Design: Terence Petryshyn